About the author

R ichard Glover is the author of five books, and three stage shows, including *Lone Star Lemon*. Richard's weekly column has appeared in the *Sydney Morning Herald* since 1985. He presents the Drive show on ABC Radio in Sydney.

In Bed
with
Jocasta

RICHARD GLOVER

HarperCollins*Publishers*

HarperCollins*Publishers*

First published in Australia in 2000
by HarperCollins*Publishers* Pty Limited
ABN 36 009 913 517
A member of HarperCollins*Publishers* (Australia) Pty Limited Group
http://www.harpercollins.com.au

HarperCollins*Publishers*
25 Ryde Road, Pymble, Sydney, NSW 2073, Australia
31 View Road, Glenfield, Auckland 10, New Zealand
77–85 Fulham Palace Road, London W6 8JB, United Kingdom
Hazelton Lanes, 55 Avenue Road, Suite 2900, Toronto, Ontario M5R 3L2
and 1995 Markham Road, Scarborough, Ontario M1B 5M8, Canada
10 East 53rd Street, New York NY 10022, USA

National Library of Australia Cataloguing-in-Publication data:

Glover, Richard.
In bed with Jocasta.
ISBN 0 7322 6864 8
1. Australian wit and humor.
2. Australia – social life and customs – Humor.
I. Title.
A828.302

Cover design: Darian Causby, HarperCollins Design Studio
Cover photograph: Australian Picture Library/Michael Wray
Printed in Australia by Griffin Press Pty Ltd on 70gsm Ensobelle

5 4 3 2 1
03 02 01 00

For Debra

Acknowledgments

The author would like to thank Debra Oswald, Amanda Higgs, Brian Curran, Linda Funnell and Belinda Yuille.

Contents

Three

Four

Five

Six

Seven

Eight

Introduction

I don't know whether to describe what follows as a comedy book, or just the world's weirdest love story. The main character is my partner who, as you will read, is formidable.

This book is also about turning forty, flirting, cooking, and being a Girl Magnet.

In order to avoid legal action, the wife character is called Jocasta. I have spent many years trying to convince the newspaper-reading public of her unfair ways and fierce nature.

Alas, she grows more popular with her every outrage.

Women, I've been told, have taken to quoting her behaviour, with some suggesting she is some sort of *go-girl* role model.

Hopefully, with the length afforded by a book, I can finally white-ant this emerging fan base, and fully catalogue her crimes.

Not that I don't enjoy being with her. Especially *in bed* with her.

I first met Jocasta when I was twenty-one. I was pimply and unattractive, and she did things in bed that no other woman was willing to do.

For instance: staying *in* the bed when I hopped into it. It certainly set her apart from the others.

I hope you enjoy our adventures in the years since. Particularly, any mention of our two children.

They have negotiated a deal which pays them $1 for every mention. The least you could do is laugh. As for Jocasta, she has eschewed any payment, but simply wishes it noted: the real Debra is much, much nicer than the fictional Jocasta.

Although — natch — just as sexy.

So, if you have a true love, and a weird life that looks normal — but only to passing outsiders — you might enjoy this book.

It may be the world's strangest love story or things just as weird might be happening in your household right now.

Frankly, I suspect it.

1

'On what *possible* grounds,' says Jocasta
as the credits roll, 'did you think it would
be pornographic?'

I go to bed defeated. I am fed up with
Hollywood. Disenchanted with the Finns.
And let down by the Australian
Censorship Board.

The Joy of Passing Wind

'It's Finnish,' says Jocasta. 'Wasn't that some sort of tip-off?'

I'm standing in the living room, wondering what the Finns ever did to Jocasta. Why this anger? Why this emotion?

'Plus,' she says, hitting the rewind button, 'it's the fourth time in a row. Four times I let you go to the video store, and four times the result is an absolute stinker.'

I feel she's being a bit unfair on *Drifting Clouds*, the Finnish movie we've just finished watching. For a start, she insists on calling it '*Passing Wind*'.

'Look on the box of *Passing Wind*,' says Jocasta, 'and you can see all the warning signs. "Sumptuously photographed" — that means there's no plot. And "deadpan humour" — that means it's a festival for misery-gutses.'

I try to remember what made me reach for it at the video store. The sticker claiming some vague connection with the Cannes Film Festival? The rave review from the

Helsinki Sanamat? The promise that the movie 'will leave you delighted and happy'?

('That,' says Jocasta, 'is the mere relief at its being over.')

There are always five or six of us at the video store, walking up and down, staring at the new releases. We may look like lost souls, condemned to wander and pause and wander again, but really we're full of hope.

This time we're going to choose something wonderful — an undiscovered gem, a real surprise. We'll take it home like an offering and, at the end of the movie, our partners will lean over with a grateful kiss. 'You've done it again,' they'll say, 'that was just wonderful.'

But it never quite works out like that.

Every week, at the end of the film, Jocasta and I have the discussion. 'On what *possible* grounds,' she asks, 'did you think it would be good?'

'Well, what about this review?' I say, pointing to the word 'hilarious' in big print.

Says Jocasta, pointing to the small print: 'Do you generally base your cultural decisions on those of Chattanooga Radio KWYZ?'

'Or what about this?' I say gamely. 'The *Scunthorpe Gazette* said it was "thought-provoking".'

'Yeah,' says Jocasta, 'provoking the thought: "Why do I ever let my dickhead husband choose the video?".'

The next week I'm back there, wandering the aisles. Never again, I mumble to myself, will I trust Chattanooga Radio KWYZ. So all those videos are off my list. Plus movies recommended by the *Scunthorpe Gazette*. Plus anything vaguely Finnish.

This time, I think, I'll base it on track record. This film says it's got the same Best Boy as *The Big Chill*; and this one is from the caterer that brought us *Romeo and Juliet*. I make my selection. I take it home. And, afterwards, we have the discussion.

'On what *possible* grounds,' says Jocasta, 'did you think it would be good?'

I read from the box: 'It's from the actor that brought us *Dirty Dancing*.'

'And,' says Jocasta, completing my sentence, 'hasn't made a good film since.'

She reaches for the video and slips it back into the box. 'There are rules for these things. For a start, you should always ignore any film which combines three famous actors with a title you've never heard of. With a cast like that, there's got to be a reason it sank without trace. Also, when they say "beautifully acted and directed" it's because they forgot to include a plot. And when the box mentions the special effects, or the soundtrack or the stunts, it means it has nothing else going for it. OK?'

'OK,' I affirm.

I return to the shop. I wander the aisles. Finnish films: out. Anything recommended by an American radio station: out. Ditto: Patrick Swayze. Finally, I've got it. My skin prickles with delight. If I'm unable to pick a film that's got some quality to it, at least I could get something *rude*.

Forget the reviews. Forget the stars. Forget Finland. This time my choice will be entirely based on the censorship rating.

This one has a very provocative cover, but I notice the Australian Censorship Board was utterly unimpressed. 'Low Level Sex Scenes,' it says, its disappointment obvious. Another film on offer can only manage Occasional Obscene Language.

Finally I make my choice. High Level Sex Scenes. Drug Use. Really Bad Language. This film has got it all. I take it home.

Late that night, giggling with expectation, we begin watching, Jocasta nuzzling closer to me, her finger tracing a lazy pattern on my chest.

'On what *possible* grounds,' says Jocasta ninety minutes later, as the credits roll, 'did you think it would be pornographic?'

I go to bed defeated. I am disappointed with Chattanooga radio KWYZ. Fed up with Hollywood. Disenchanted with the Finns. And let down by the Australian Censorship Board. All in all, *Passing Wind* now doesn't seem so bad.

'Maybe I pre-judged it,' says Jocasta. 'Shall we get it out again?'

Mauled

'All the jobs, done in one day. We'll knock off the lot,' says Jocasta as we drive towards the local Mega Mall, the kids already fighting over who gets to hold the shopping list. It's Saturday morning, and we're going on a journey, as many people have before us. For instance: Dante.

9.00 We're in Ikea, and already The Space Cadet is swinging on a hat stand named Klug. All the products have insistently Swedish names. The couch is called Toj, the desk is Brok and the lamp is Blag — names that sound like members of ABBA. Hopefully, I'll soon have my bum in a Bjorn, and my feet on a collapsible Frida.

9.20 We need a lamp for the lounge, and compare the five on offer — the Tovik, Skimpa, Bodge, Blag and Barf. These are not the sweet sounds of home-making. These are the sounds of gastro-intestinal distress. Finally, Jocasta asks the sales assistant if she can have a Barf. But the Barfs are all sold out.

9.30 I prise The Space Cadet off a tent called Pog, and chase him and Batboy out of the store. Jocasta and I discuss the way all our society's virtues have been turned into product names. Praise is a margarine, Kindness is a soap, Courage a lipstick. And now, just like Nelson Mandela, we must begin our long walk to Freedom.

9.40 We stumble into Freedom Furniture. It's a store with no Swedish connection, yet the names still sound like Terge and Flurg. Is this the cultural cringe? Why not a couch called Barry, an umbrella stand named Tony, or, for that matter, a poof named Adrian? We proceed to the lighting section. While Freedom may light the path ahead (especially in its outdoors section), it cannot tastefully light our lounge.

9.50 Depression is setting in. In quick succession, we visit Suzie's World of Lights, Mr Lighting, and The Light Master. All have well-developed ideas of style and restraint: ideas derived from those of Mr Elvis Presley, Las Vegas, circa 1969.

10.10 'We'll give up on the lamp,' says Jocasta grumpily, and so we move onto Item Two on the list: the birthday presents for the boy and girl in The Space Cadet's class.

10.30 Visit Toys U Buy, Mr Toys, and World of Crap. Large quantities of extruded plastic tosh have been packaged into brightly coloured boxes, helpfully coded as to gender. Everything in the store, however small, appears to cost $29.95. Except for the stuff that costs $149.95. Purchase 2 kilos of blue crap, and 2.5 kilos of pink crap. Load into car.

10.40 Item Three is a chest of drawers for The Space Cadet. Naturally, we head straight for Cheap and Nasty World ('the store where the repayments *always* last longer than the product'). Everyone here is exactly our age, with exactly two kids and exactly no money. We're all hoping that by the time this stuff falls apart, we'll be able to afford better — although, looking at the products and at the customers, this seems unlikely. We buy 35 kilos of flat-pack chipboard, which has been vaguely glued together into the shape of drawers.

11.29 We leave Cheap and Nasty World ('where we're confident to stand on our reputation — but never our chairs') and get caught in a surge of people. It's a river of parents and hungry children, all marching towards Mr Hamburger World. We end up at the counter, and place our orders. Somehow, it reminds me of Cheap and Nasty World and Toys 4 Profit. The food is pre-digested, extruded, portion-controlled. It's soft and easy to chew, almost as if someone has already digested it. That thought has implications, and I fight them off.

12.00 The kids are depressed, and so are we. Somehow Batboy talks us into a visit to Time-Waste-Zone, the game arcade. Apparently, if you spend $20, you may very well win a piece of plastic crap. Batboy and I have a go on the skiing machine, which is — in its way — quite amazing. There's a video screen, and skis and stocks. For $2, it is a little bit like skiing.

Just like The Space Cadet's furniture is a little bit like furniture.

And the plastic crap is a little like a real toy.

And the hamburger is a little like real food.

And the lights are a little like something attractive.

Which brings us back to Dante. Like him, we're now ready to go home. Travelling back, through all seven circles of the modern world.

The Mouse Trap

The Space Cadet wants a pet. He suggests a large dog, and is met with fierce opposition. He moderates to a cat, and does no better.

'A guinea pig?' he asks quietly a week later, cutting the cloth of his dreams into ever-smaller pieces. Unbelievably, his mean-hearted father still says no. The Space Cadet turns sadly, his shoulders fallen, and limps back into his bedroom.

At this rate, he'll be asking for a pet flea within a month, and still be getting knock-backs. And so I say it, mumbling towards his departing back: 'Maybe a mouse.'

The Space Cadet embraces the idea with an enthusiasm bordering on hysteria. 'A mouse would be *fantastic*,' he says. 'I've always wanted a mouse. Always.'

I tell him that I'm not going to give in straight away. He must prove he *really* wants a mouse. On the spot I come up with an excellent parenting idea: he can have the mouse if he remembers to ask again, once a week for, say, three weeks.

But The Space Cadet doesn't have a great grip on the calendar. He's so nervous about missing the deadline, he decides to take precautions, and asks me about the mouse every five minutes, every day, for ten straight days.

Finally I crack. We drive to the shop, and The Space Cadet is shaking in his seat with the excitement of it all. His first pet.

'Which floor of Ashfield Mall do you reckon the pet shop'll be on?' Jocasta asks, and The Space Cadet answers her: 'It'll be on the ground floor.'

We ask him how he knows. Says The Space Cadet, jiggling as he talks: 'Well, they'd put it on the ground floor because the children really want the pets. And if it's on the ground floor they can go in and get the pets *really* quickly.'

We arrive at the mall and walk into the pet shop, which is on the ground floor. We find this allows us to get separated from our money *really* quickly.

The Space Cadet selects a mouse, and then a mouse cage. The mouse costs $2. The cage, which is on special, costs $49.95. It is made of brightly coloured plastic, and features a sort of Centrepoint Tower rising up from its top, up which the mouse can climb.

When we get home, The Space Cadet announces that the mouse is called Fluffy, and we all sit around the kitchen table watching him as he runs on his wheel.

'Fluffy is very fast,' says The Space Cadet, and we all agree. We've chanced upon an exceptional mouse. Perhaps the fastest, most athletic mouse ever. We all decide we're very proud of him.

Steve, from over the road, wanders in and watches Fluffy on his treadmill, going ever round and round and round, and becomes increasingly depressed. 'It's like a metaphor,' he says grimly before wandering out into the back garden and staring into the distance.

His partner, Helen, says she doesn't like the mouse, but the mouse house, with its neon-bright plastic tower, and 'Lazy Vue' viewing platform, would make the basis of an excellent building application to council, and would we mind if she took a few measurements?

The Space Cadet, though, just wants to get Fluffy out, and have him crawl up his arm, holding his tail as demonstrated by the lady in the shop. We do this successfully. Three times. But not the fourth.

Fluffy escapes. We've had him precisely five hours, and are now owners of a perfectly useless $49.95 plastic mouse cage, with Lazy Vue platform and neon-bright tower.

Batboy says that since a $2 mouse lives two years; maybe next time we could get a $4 mouse, which would live four years.

The Space Cadet is looking glum. 'We don't even know when his birthday is,' he says, as if this makes the loss all the more hurtful.

Jocasta is even more upset. 'I'd already bonded to Fluffy,' she says miserably.

I spot some movement. Fluffy is under the couch. The last time we had a mouse under the couch my intentions were rather more deadly. This time, it's different. With four planks of wood we construct a sort of stockyard around the couch, and consider how to lift out the furniture.

I summon various helpers, and soon we have five adults, arguing over the capture options.

'Don't hurt him,' says The Space Cadet.

'Yeah,' says Steve, who's stalked back inside from the garden, 'we should subdue him first with capsicum spray.'

In the end we lift out the couch, work in the barriers, and successfully return Fluffy to his owner. He seems happy enough to be crawling over The Space Cadet, who, this time, maintains a somewhat better grip on his tail.

Back on his treadmill, Fluffy runs faster than ever, as Jocasta watches with a gasp of admiration. 'What a mouse. An exceptional mouse.'

My Mother Killed My Stove

Suddenly, all the battles of childhood are over. After forty years of losing every argument with my mother, I've got the goods on her. She has come to Sydney and cleaned our cooktop to death. She has killed it armed with nothing more than a pump-pack of Spray and Wipe and an over-zealous attitude to germs.

Of course, all mothers think their children live in filthy hovels. But not many have actually cleaned one of their son's appliances to death — squirting in so much Spray and Wipe that the house is plunged into darkness each time we turn on the hotplate.

Of course, we were expecting her visit. 'My mother's coming to stay,' I said to Jocasta a week ago, and watched her eyes flicker with fear as she reached for the nearest Wettex.

My mother usually arrives from the country wearing white cotton gloves — designed to ward off the germs of the city in general, and our house in particular. Does she have the cleanliness problem, or do we? Is she compulsively clean, bordering on clinical insanity? Or are we animals who live in our own filth? It's an open question; but certainly standards are different.

In our last house Jocasta finally snapped, accused my mother of suffering from Obsessive Compulsive Disorder, and advised her to invest in some sort of psychiatric medication. My mother replied that she was happy as she was and suggested that, since advice was being handed around, Jocasta might like to invest in a new Wettex.

Who won that particular battle of wills? I find it difficult to assess the evidence at the moment, especially with all the noise of Jocasta simultaneously vacuuming the hall rug with one hand while she dusts off the bookshelves with the other.

In between, Jocasta is yelling instructions at the rest of us. She says I've got to finish the bathroom and then move on to the stove — getting it so clean, Mum won't be tempted to reach into the cupboard for the Spray and Wipe as soon as she arrives.

'I'm not attacking your family,' says Jocasta. 'All I'm saying is that when your father comes we have to hide all the grog, and when your mother comes we have to hide all the cleaning products.'

We clean for two days solid, at which point my mother arrives. Despite our efforts, I can see her having to steady herself as she gets her first glance at the kitchen.

'It's lovely, darling,' she says, pulling on her white gloves that little bit more tightly. She wanders around the house, using that tone of false brightness which is reserved for mothers viewing their son's life choices.

My mother's problem with germs has certainly been around for a while. At age eight, my career in the Boy Scouts was cut short after I telephoned my mother from the bush adventure camp and mentioned there was nowhere to wash my hands after going to the toilet.

'Don't move, I'll be right there,' she said, before sprinting to the car and driving the four hours up the highway, spinning into the camp car park with dust flying.

'Why are you going back to Sydney?' yelled the other boys, shouting after the departing car.

'To wash my hands,' I yelled back.

All these years later, it's not me, but Batboy and The Space Cadet who are receiving the wisdom of her instruction. Batboy, for one, has turned into a bit of a recruit. 'You know, dad,' he admonishes, toothbrush in hand, his mouth frothing like a rabid dog, 'you really need to scrub for at least five minutes to get them *properly* clean.'

The Space Cadet, though, is a different matter.

Jocasta and I leave early for work, and so The Gloved-One takes the job of giving him breakfast. It doesn't go well.

The Space Cadet refuses to eat his toast, so my mother decides to use some of her advanced parenting techniques. The ones which have left me such a well-balanced and stable person.

She walks into the room, stands in front of The Space Cadet and pretends to cry. 'If you don't eat your toast,' she tells him, sniffling, 'I'll get in trouble with your daddy. And then I'll cry and cry.'

Returning to the room some minutes later, she sees the plate is empty. 'Good boy! You've eaten it all up!'

'Well, no,' says The Space Cadet, a glint in his seven-year-old eyes. 'I *want* you to get in trouble with Daddy. So I've hidden it.'

The Gloved-One begs and pleads. But The Space Cadet is resolute.

For the last days of her visit, she knows it is out there: somewhere dark and out of sight, the Lost Toast, festering away, shooting its spores of germs into the air. For someone with a germ phobia, it is *torture*.

We mount search parties, The Space Cadet sitting silent, thrilled with his power, Batboy crawling around, staring under chairs, my mother looking distracted, her fingers nervously plucking the edge of her gloves.

All in all, it's little wonder she took it all out on the cooktop — cleaning it into electrical oblivion. Whatever the repair fees, I feel it's worth it.

A day after her departure, The Space Cadet languidly reaches behind the back wheel of the couch, and pulls out the piece of toast. He gives me a restrained smile, and drops it in the bin.

Looking back at my childhood, I don't think I was ever much of a match for my mother. But I've had a hand in raising someone who is.

Yes, We're Australian

Every tourist guide to Australia has an extensive guide to Australian slang — defining words like cobber, cossie and fair dinkum. Yet the truly unique things — our cultural rules and tribal beliefs — are left undocumented.

If our visitors really want to fit in, here's what they'll need to know:

1. The bigger the hat, the smaller the farm.
2. The shorter the nickname they give you, the more they like you.
3. It's not a genuine Australian saying unless it involves a paddock, a lizard or a rat.
4. A flash sports car driven by a middle-aged man does not incite envy — as it does in America — but hilarity.
5. It's not a picnic without a bull-ant climbing up your bum.
6. It is proper to refer to your best friend as 'a total bastard', but your worst enemy as 'a *bit* of a bastard'.
7. Whether it's the opening of Parliament, or the launch of a new art gallery, there is no event

which cannot be improved by the addition of a sausage sizzle.

8. All banks are bastards.

9. A hamburger must contain beetroot.

10. It's considered better to be down on your luck than up yourself.

11. The phrase 'we've got a great lifestyle' means everyone in the family drinks too much.

12. If the guy next to you is swearing like a wharfie, he's probably a media billionaire. Or, just conceivably, a wharfie.

13. There is no food that cannot be improved by the application of tomato sauce.

14. People with red hair should be nicknamed 'Blue', just as short people should be labelled 'Lofty'.

15. On the beach, all Australians hide their keys and wallet by placing them inside their sandshoes. No thief has ever worked this out. We may have very stupid thieves. Or *really* stinky sandshoes.

16. Industrial design knows of no article more useful than the milk crate.

17. All our best heroes are losers.

18. The Alpha male in any group is he who takes the barbecue tongs from the hands of the host, and blithely begins turning the snags.

19. It's not summer until the steering wheel is too hot to hold.

20. Beer should be served so cold it makes your ears hurt.

21. A thong is not a piece of scanty swimwear, as in America, but a fine example of footwear.

A group of sheilas wearing black rubber thongs may not be as exciting as you had hoped.

22. A gum leaf, crushed, in the hand, is the best smell ever.

23. There shall be no dobbers.

24. Historians believe the widespread use of the word 'mate' can be traced to the harsh conditions on the Australian frontier in the 1890s, and the development of a code of mutual aid, or 'mateship'. Alternatively, we may all be just really hopeless with names.

25. The wise man chooses a partner who is attractive not only to himself, but also to neighbourhood mosquitoes.

26. If it can't be fixed using panty-hose and fencing wire, it's not worth fixing.

27. All parties, in however grand and well-prepared a house, shall be held, cramped and noisy, in the kitchen.

28. The most popular and widely praised family in any street is the one that just happens to have the swimming pool.

29. A swallowed fly, while disgusting, must be greeted with the plucky comment: 'Mmm, protein.'

30. We invented everything in the world worth inventing, but then sold the patent to the Yanks.

31. Smearing toast with a spread that's black and salty, and which has the appearance of axle-grease, is widely viewed as a good way to start the day.

32. Every older Australian has a bullshit theory involving ants, a kookaburra laughing and the likelihood of rain, and every theory is the direct opposite of the last one you heard.

33. If invited to a party, you should take cheap red wine, but then spend all night drinking the host's beer. Don't worry: he'll have catered for it.

34. The phrase 'a simple picnic' is not known. Or at least not acted upon. You should take *everything*. If you don't need to make three trips back to car, you are not trying.

35. If there's any sort of free event or party within a hundred kilometres, you'd be a mug not to go.

36. A kid, upon burying his father in the sand, shall always give him breasts larger than those of his mother.

37. Every surname, brand-name and motor-car spare part must be shortened to the point of incomprehension, as in the sentence: 'If I hadn't stuffed the diff, I'd have taken Blacky to Maccas.'

38. There comes a time in every Australian's life when he or she realises that the Aeroguard is far, far worse than the flies.

39. Our national character means that we cry during the first verse of our national anthem, but can't remember the words of the rest.

40. And, finally, don't let the tourist books fool you. No one says 'cobber'.

Helpful? No worries!

Rat-bagged

In the school science curriculum of the mid–1970s, it was mandatory to dissect a rat at every opportunity. If your teacher wanted to explain water evaporation in the Murray–Darling basin, he'd work in some sort of rat dissection. Ask him the atomic weight of magnesium, and the answer would come back: 'Hand me a rat.'

It was even worse in my class, because my teacher was using rat dissection as part of a long-term scientific project — trying to establish just how many times he could, via rat dissection, cause me to faint or throw up.

Actually, I fainted only once, but that one faint was so spectacular, so breathtakingly humiliating, that you could understand the teacher's desire to see the moment repeated. (This, of course, was in the days before the Internet, so teachers had to make their own fun.)

The occasion was a lecture about the dangers of heroin abuse, in which the teacher, quite naturally, took the opportunity to dissect a rat. This, he said, was in order to show us the intricate wonders of the human body — a task which, speaking personally, I felt was more easily achieved in French class in idle contemplation of Madame Chabrol.

But, for him, it had to be the rat, which he had pinned to a board and was just pointing out the wonders of the little lungs when I sought permission to 'go to the bathroom'. Permission granted, I strode manfully towards the door, teetered a little in front of the teacher's desk, turned a sharp shade of white, and then fell face forward onto the floor.

How long did I stay there, unconscious? Reports were uncertain — muffled as they were by the sound of thirty-two classmates pissing themselves with laughter. What's clear is that I remain very worried by any mention of rodents.

The rodents who last week invaded our kitchen are mice rather than rats, but still there's the sensation that total humiliation cannot be far off. For a start, The Space Cadet has to be convinced they are a totally different species to his pet mouse Fluffy, who continues to gambol — oblivious — on his Lazy Vue viewing platform.

Over a week, I set about twenty traps, twelve of which fail to go off (the mice regarding them largely as serving platters for that day's cheesy offering); seven of which slam shut, but on top of my fingers; and one of which — no doubt due to some freakish accident — actually kills a mouse.

Which is when Locky arrives to stay.

Locky is our mate from the bush, a rice farmer who wears genuine bush boots and a genuine bush hat and can build a tractor engine using nothing but a roll of chook wire and a pair of old socks. On all indications, he is the sort of bloke unlikely to have fainted during science class.

'What would *you* do about our mice plague?' says Jocasta, instantly cheering to the thought that at last the house has a *proper* bloke in it.

'Yes, what would you do, Locky?' says Batboy, pausing in his drooling admiration of Locky's hat.

And so Locky launches into three hours of increasingly unlikely bush stories in which he single-handedly defeats ever larger armies of mice, right up to the story of how the mice lifted his whole barn and carried it into Deniliquin and Locky had to carry it back. All of which is told as Jocasta, Batboy and The Space Cadet form a small and ever-more-adoring circle, demanding details of the trap that finally defeated the mice.

'Ah,' said Locky, 'it was a traditional bush trap.'

And so Locky described it, while Batboy, following his instructions, built the thing.

I felt sorry for Locky really; it was such a stupid contraption, like something a kid would dream up. It featured an empty beer bottle, lying on a shelf, its neck sticking over the edge, a piece of cheese shoved in its mouth, and a bucket of water below. An old sock (there's always an old sock in Locky's contraptions) goes over the big end of the bottle, and the neck is greased with butter. The mouse — sure, Locky, sure — will walk along the bottle, towards the cheese, using the traction of the sock, step onto the butter, fall, then drown in the water.

All in all, a daft idea and proof once again of the tragic fantasy world in which many of our farmers are now living. Indeed, as we sat round the dinner table I started advising Locky how he needed to spend more time in town, updating his ideas, trying to get more of a grip on reality, which was exactly when we heard the first plop.

One drowned mouse. The first of eight caught since in The Locky Trap.

Only trouble is, Locky's gone home now, so it's up to me to reach into the water and fish out the little dead bodies, turning as I do it various shades of blue, green and yellow. And up to me to turn Fluffy's mouse house discreetly away.

Have I fainted yet? Surprisingly, no. Could it be that The Locky Trap is finally making a man of me?

About-to-Expire Eggs

When I was sixteen and living alone with my father, the culinary standard was not high. For breakfast we would both have two raw eggs, stirred up in a glass of milk with a fork — me adding a spoonful of chocolate Quik as a concession to youth. For dinner we would have lamb chops, done under the griller, served with mashed potato and frozen peas.

We would have this meal on Mondays. Then we'd have it on Tuesdays. On Wednesdays. On Thursdays. And on Fridays. From this distance, I can't recall the weekends, but I have a strong suspicion they involved chops, potatoes and peas. I also remember thinking the whole thing very tasty.

Jamie Oliver, the Naked Chef, has reached the bestseller lists by promoting the simplicity of his recipes — but he's nothing on my dad. Or on a thousand other suburban chefs. They have *really* simple recipes. Perhaps it's time someone recorded their subtle joys.

Ted's Lamb Chops and Mash

Buy 10 kilos of lamb chops and place in the freezer. Each day, before work, remove six chops and defrost. Place under griller until burnt. Serve with mash, peas and lashing of tomato sauce. Beautiful! (Hint: if special guests are attending dinner, why not chop a tomato in half and also bung under the griller.)

Back-of-Cupboard Bake

Jamie Oliver loves choosing ingredients from the same region — and so do we. In particular: the region at the very back of the cupboard.

Step 1: Root around in there, pulling out every canned product you can find, and open the lot.
Step 2: Check at least two of them are soup. If not, add water.
Step 3: Pour over Deb Mashed Potato, and cook until hot, or until phone rings with better offer.

About-to-Expire Eggs

Jamie Oliver says one should be guided by what's fresh on one's daily visit to the markets. We take rather the opposite approach: preferring to be guided according to what's in our fridge and about to expire. About-to-Expire Eggs, On-The-Turn Mince, and Get-in-Quick Lasagne all involve a commitment from the whole family: you'll knock off the lot tonight. And hope.

Twice-Dropped Sausages

Jamie offers Twice-Cooked Duck, but it's hardly as simple as twice-dropped snags. In this recipe, the snag is first dropped off the side of the grill into the barbecue itself, thus picking up a generous coating of ash, and is then — just before serving — dropped on the kitchen floor, thus picking up subtle Asian influences, themselves twice-dropped during last night's stir fry. It's a recipe so good, you'll never want to reveal its secrets.

Chinese Take-Away Reheat

A robust dish in which one can travel all the regions of China within a single mouthful. Simply consolidate all last-night's left-overs into one microwavable dish, stirring to ensure the sweet and sour pork is well distributed through the prawn soup. (Internationalists may also like to include the slice of pizza left over from Wednesday.)
Step 1: Cook quickly.
Step 2: Eat rapidly.
Step 3: Regret at leisure.

Cling-Wrap Combination

If it's in the fridge, sealed with either cling-wrap or a clothes peg, it should be on this delightfully eclectic platter. Wedges of cheese, slightly suspect salami, a single piece of soccerball ham with dried-up edges, three tomatoes with the bad bits cut off, and five broken Saos. And to think the Italians claim to have invented antipasto! *Mi scusi*, Mario: we've had it for years.

Mick's Fry-Up

My friend Mick believes that if it's food, then you should be able to fry it. Especially after a big night out, when the human body craves the soothing balm that is cholesterol. Chops, eggs, bacon, kippers, chicken kebabs, tomatoes, mushrooms and bread — according to Mick — all yearn to be flung into a pan with a large quantity of butter. Yet, like many of Jamie Oliver's recipes, this one takes some preparation.

Step 1: Go to pub the night before, and marinate own brain in alcohol, being careful to top up levels should any drying-out occur.

Step 2: Awake with shocking hangover.

Step 3: Remove entire contents of fridge and fry in butter.

Step 4: Eat until consciousness returns.

Step 5: Serve single glass of orange juice, thus rendering healthy all your behaviour of the last twelve hours.

Fridge-Light Dessert

A delightfully simple recipe, this is the way dessert is served in most households, on most nights. Each diner should approach the fridge during a separate

TV ad break and, standing in the illumination of the opened door, root around until they find something worth eating. A square of cooking chocolate, an abandoned Easter egg, the crusty dregs from a carton of readymade custard. If questioned by other diners, you should rapidly swallow, and deny you were up to anything.

As tasty as Jamie's Lemon and Lime Cream Tart? Perhaps not, but truly *wicked*.

2

Then she sighs. It's a long, bleak sigh, slipping from her lips with a mixture of exhaustion and self-pity. As best I can decode it, it contains within it the narrative of how, twenty years ago, an intelligent young woman with options in life made a series of decisions which led her, in middle-age, to be driving at 30 kilometres an hour over the Anzac Bridge with a moron.

Vice Squad

In the building trade, everything has some bizarre, slightly Yorkshire-sounding name, designed to cause humiliation once you arrive at the hardware store.

'Hey George,' the main bloke will yell out, shouting down to his wizened offsider at the back. 'Guess what this bloke wants to do? He's going to use a crumpin pin to fix his nondles.' At which point, thirty tradesman in overalls will turn to face the counter, in their excitement sending flying to the floor countless packets of scrogin bolts, grommet flanges and grogan pipes.

'He's got his nondles mixed up with his scrogins,' they chorus as one, laughing merrily, and lurch into a little dance, all the while casting admiring glances at each other's spondles.

Sometimes, watching them, I'd like to insert a grogan into each of their blurgin pipes. Except, of course, for the ever-increasing price of grogans.

I'm only here, in the hardware store, because large cracks have just appeared in our new bathroom floor — the bathroom floor I've only just finished installing. Plus the toilet creaks every time you come near it.

It seems I stuffed-up the level of the joists when I rebuilt the floor. Which means that each time you approach the toilet you're greeted by a loud and apprehensive moan.

Jocasta calls it the 'talking toilet' and says we should have hired a tradesman. She's right. The joists are stuffed, but so are the bearers, the soffets, the tindrills, the blagdorms, the rafters and the reefers.

Mind you, it was Jocasta who encouraged this current spate of DIY — or Destroy-It-Yourself, as we now call it. She's the one who bought me the portable workbench, designed to clamp wood or piping at various angles, and costing a fortune. A fortune so great that, finally, in mid-life, I realised I'd become a man with expensive vices.

The portable bench has some sort of fancy marketing name, like the Bloke-O-Matic or the Handi Guy. It's solitary. It's portable. It's a vice. And yet it's still approved by the Vatican.

The only catch is that the Bloke-O-Matic is supplied in bits in a flat-pack box, and it emerges that you need a Bloke-O-Matic and about $500 worth of tools in order to put it together. But, still, some people have been lucky enough to somehow manoeuvre Bolt E into Hole C and end up with something featuring four intertwined legs and two vices (remember: still Vatican approved).

And it's only natural that these people believe they can do anything. Even build a bathroom.

Which is how I found myself digging trenches for the sewerage pipe and considering the need for some new building regulations, specifically designed for the nation's Do-It-Yourselfers. Such as:

Regulation 1: By all means, blame your tools

I'm sorry, it's not just that we are bad tradesmen: our tools are stuffed. I couldn't help what happened with the joists. I do not own a proper carpenter's plane. They cost $65. Which is why I tried to plane the joists using a chainsaw. (This, I swear, is true.) It's a measure of my skill that the levels are not out by more.

Regulation 2: Mistakes multiply

When you look at our work, sure, you think we're idiots; that no-one could do a job this bad. Just remember: mistakes multiply. The bathroom's a disaster because the ridge beam is two degrees out. Which is why the tin didn't fit. Which is why the guttering looked odd. Which is why the walls weren't straight. If I had better tools ...

Regulation 3: It's not the roof of the Sistine Chapel

Or the walls. Or the floor. In other words, 'after a while you won't care'. The welcoming groan of the talking toilet is like the song of a bird, signalling the start of the day. The wonderfully madcap tiling is a delight. The gaps in the skirting boards are a chance to experience the sweet breezes of early spring.

Regulation 4: There's a brand-name product for every task

And, given men's fear of reading instructions, the manufacturers usually bury a guide-to-using-it right there in the title. Brand names such as Sticks Real Fast. Or Spray on Quick. Or, my personal favourite, Selley's No More Cracks — a pair of elastic-waisted work pants, guaranteed never to ride down, even when you're crouching to get under the sink.

Regulation 5: Measure twice, cut once

Well, that's the old rule but, for reasons of space, they never printed the full DIY version: 'Measure twice, cut once, try to install, find it still doesn't fit, throw board to the ground, shout at partner, buy new bit at hardware store, endure sarcasm because you hadn't realised you really need a blondgit bolt, cut again, and install.'

Perhaps you don't believe anybody can be this stupid? Why not come over to my place and see the big stack of treated pine, all of it cut to 1.2 metres in length (for a pergola designed to be 1.4 metres).

Back at the hardware store, the men have removed their leather aprons, and are dancing around a large display of metric grogans, their spondles aquiver. I'd love to join them, yet my solitary vice calls me home.

Travel Sickness

Batboy has discovered that his mum's new computer is fitted with a DVD player. Sitting on her floor, with the speakers just right, it's like the ultimate cinema experience. He's also discovered that you can watch the film with German subtitles — thus qualifying as language homework.

Alas, we've only got one DVD film — a copy of *The Birdcage*, the Robin Williams comedy about a gay couple whose son marries into the Moral Majority. I fear the lad is developing a somewhat specialised vocabulary — *Schwulen im Militär* (gays in the military); *Abtreibungsarzt* (abortion doctor) and *Transvestitenklub* (transvestites' club).

My question is: are these terms which will come up on the Year 7 exams?

Maybe I should buy a different sort of movie — one with lots of talk about putting your pen on the desk of your teacher before opening the window (or *Fenster*). Going on the evidence of his German lesson-book, in Deutschland they talk of little else.

It is important, during this difficult week, that Batboy 'self-motivates' during his homework. Jocasta is away working in Melbourne yet again, and I've got to cut a few corners.

True, being a momentary single parent has one advantage: it allows you to drink what you like at night. As early as Monday night, however, a small gem of wisdom begins to form: this is not always particularly helpful.

Worse, Jocasta has left me a list. It's a highly offensive document which implies I know nothing about the running of the house. She has stuck it on the fridge, with bold capitals listing each day of the week. It seeks to guide my every waking moment, from 'make sandwiches' at 6.45 a.m., right up to 'put soccer boots in back of car for tomorrow' at 11.15 p.m.

My eyes feverishly search for some more upbeat tasks: '8.30 p.m. Sprawl on couch, drunk, watching movie'; or '10.15 p.m. Slip out and have hot affair'. Remarkably, these things are not listed.

Besides which, as I tell Jocasta before she goes, the list is unnecessary and I won't look at it once. I tell her: 'If I ever go away for a week, *then* we'll need a list. A list of all the things *I* do.'

Says Jocasta: 'What will you use for paper, Cinderella? A Post-it note?'

By day two, we're running so late that Batboy has missed the bus to school, and I have to drive him. We get there half an hour late. Batboy is unimpressed.

'What are you trying to do, Dad?' he says, getting out of the car. 'Turn me into a *nervöses Wrack*?'

I make a mental note: get that boy a new film.

Wednesday, and Jocasta rings up. The Space Cadet gets to the phone and launches into a long account of how he didn't have his recorder in his bag for music because 'Dad forgot it'.

I make a mental note: explain to The Space Cadet that no-one likes a dobber.

I get onto the phone. Jocasta says: 'You know the recorder was on the list. Are you following the list?' Something about the way she says it, makes me realise it should be rendered in capital letters. It's now become THE LIST.

Thursday, and it appears we have run out of soccer shorts, tops and socks. I surreptitiously consult THE LIST and notice a small annotation on Tuesday, ordering their post-practice washing.

It's just before 'buy more bread', and just after 'buy present for Briony's birthday'. I wonder if Briony would be happy with ten bucks in an envelope. I've got plenty of money, especially considering all the savings I've made on bread.

I remove the wet and stinking soccer clothes from the laundry basket and suggest to Batboy he slips them on anyway. 'They'll be all right, mate,' I say. 'The other team won't want to come near you while you're wearing these.' I attempt a matey laugh.

He shoots me a disbelieving stare, and mumbles: '*Also das ist die Hölle.*' ('And so this is hell' — *The Birdcage*, Scene 8, line 5.)

Friday, and THE LIST says Jocasta will be home at 9.00 p.m. So how come she rings from the airport and says she's got an early flight and will be home in twenty minutes?

I just knew THE LIST was a worthless tissue of lies. Hysterically — *hysterisch* — all three of us start cleaning and organising. There's no way we will be finished on time.

'Are you coping, Dad?' asks Batboy kindly, as he watches me pound the pizza boxes down into the garbage.

'No, son', I say. 'I feel like I'm riding on a psychotic horse toward a burning barn.'

Batboy nods his head in agreement: 'Ah, yes, Scene 20, line 8: *"Ein psychotisches Pfred zu einem brennenden Stall reiten will".*'

Which leaves me with the question: how come the language of a hysterical farce seems so useful in this particular house?

Examine This

Just the mention of the Year 12 final exams — exams like the HSC or the VCE — is enough to make beads of sweat break out on the foreheads of most of us. Lucky for those about to enter the exam room, I'm in a position to offer some advice.

1. Don't believe *any* of your friends when they say they are not studying. They are merely trying to guarantee they won't be last in the class, by inviting you into just that role.
2. No-Doze tablets are a mistake. Past students have swallowed them with all the abandon of a Hume Highway truckie. In the resulting delirium, they have tended to answer every question in the Maths in Society paper with the phrase 'Yass to Gundagai'.
3. The Lemon Ruski, while in itself a fine beverage, cannot be considered a crucial study aid in either Russian Language or Soviet History.
4. On various occasions you may find yourself stark naked and sweating in the exam room. This is either (a) a pre-exam nightmare or (b) a rather

game attempt to finally win the attention of the invigilator and get another writing pad. Both events prove the law: seventeen cups of coffee is *too many*.

5. Feel free to use other students as *aides-mémoire*. Looking up mid-exam, the mountainous acne on the face of your friend Shazza might remind you of the devious role played by the Swiss in World War II. The horrific dandruff-storm enveloping Tony's head might, by contrast, bring to mind the importance of the winter snow in the siege of Stalingrad. And the very sight of your Maths teacher, Mr Greystains, might remind you of the dangers of wearing the same pair of pants for twenty years without dry-cleaning. (This last is not actually an exam tip, but remains a vital life lesson.)

6. Remember that many great human beings, including Sir Winston Churchill, did not do well at school. Then again, Sir Winston wasn't pinning his hopes on getting into Vet Science at Sydney Uni. Remember: positions as War Time Leader of the British tend to be thin on the ground when you've grown up in North Ryde.

7. While tattooing and body piercing have become popular of late, it is unlikely the invigilator will accept that you just happen to have Hamlet's second soliloquy branded onto your inner thigh.

8. During the exam period your parents will be uncharacteristically willing to wait on you hand and foot. By all means, be imperious. Enjoy it. *Exploit it*. Don't just ask Dad to make you a cup

of coffee; get the old boy slaving over pancakes and fresh juice, with the claim 'it's great brain food'. Torment other siblings. Demand silence elsewhere in the house. Bung on tantrums with impunity. Scatter books and coffee cups everywhere. Be a complete *bastard*. Remember, the HSC is an important coming-of-age ritual: it's when your parents decide that, yes, next year they *will* help you with the bond for a flat of your own.

9. It is a mistake to completely sacrifice personal hygiene to the needs of study. In my own Physics exam, five students succumbed to the stench of their own BO, and were later found unconscious. Only by chance did the imprint of their filthy foreheads mean that all achieved high distinctions in the multiple choice.

10. Why didn't you study earlier? Why did you waste all of Year 11, and most of Year 12? Why were you such a fool? All these thoughts may be now occurring to you. Stay calm. Exams favour those who know a few simple facts:

    • All literature is about the struggle between man and nature, with a side-order of the anguish of human existence. Phrases which can be safely used at random to describe any book include: 'a tortured account of la condition humaine'; 'the author's vivid use of language'; and 'a compelling, but original, sense of place'. And even if you've never heard of the novel or play in the literature test, you can always employ the all-purpose essay-ending: 'And so, despite a harsh view of human nature, the author believes humanity has the ability to rise to finer things — which is both its hope and its tragedy.'

- All history, meanwhile, is a result of the social and economic forces of the time — 'a time when the world was entering a period of rapid economic and social dislocation'. This phrase can be safely used even if you don't know what *century* the examiners are talking about, as the world has always been entering a period of rapid social and economic dislocation.

11. Read the paper through before you start. Only claim 'it's all Greek to me' if sitting Modern Greek. And take it from the rest of us: nothing you'll face in the rest of your life will be as horrible as this.

Home Coming

Melbourne is flat, with the roads laid out in a grid. No wonder Melburnians have fewer relationship problems than the rest of the population. In Sydney, you can get anywhere by about fifteen different routes.

It's a city laid out by people paid in rum and wearing leg irons. Look from the air, and it's been designed using a SpiroGraph. And so you have the arguments. Comenarra Parkway vs the Pacific Highway. Oxford Street vs William. Mona Vale Road vs Pittwater.

Jocasta and I may have to stop attending the Broadway cinema, so intense is our argument about which way to turn when we leave the car park. To the right and up Parramatta Road? To the left and across Anzac Bridge? Before you express a preference, let me admit it: I'm passionately in favour of the Parramatta Road option.

Jocasta sits next to me, fuming. 'I can't believe you're going this way again. It's madness.'

Mostly I ignore Jocasta's comments, but today I snap. I chuck a U-turn. Right there in the middle of the road. 'OK, you win. You direct.'

Jocasta tells me to stop being so childish, and says she was merely expressing an opinion.

I say: 'Well, we're now *following* your opinion. So it's your job to tell me where to go.'

Jocasta indicates she'd like to do exactly that.

In this sort of argument, it's best to be the driver. Jocasta is directing me towards the Anzac Bridge, and so my aim is to prove this is the slowest, most foolish route imaginable.

My eyes scan the road ahead, searching out opportunities. Slow vehicles which, by clever driving, I can get stuck behind. Buses which might stop to let off passengers. Turning lanes in which I can get myself marooned. And traffic lights which, by the imperceptible slowing of our car, I can inspire to turn red.

Jocasta says: 'You're deliberately going slow.'

I deny it. 'It's just such a *very* difficult road.'

With a sense of triumph I spot a broken-down taxi in the kerbside lane, and allow myself a victorious glance towards Jocasta. I hope the glance will convey the message: 'This sort of breakdown happens all the time on the Anzac Bridge, but never on Parramatta Road. Further proof that I am right once again.'

I realise this seems a lot of information to convey in a single glance, but you should have been there to see how I narrowed my eyes, glowered towards her, then sighed.

Yes! Sighed! (Although, a thought did bubble up: 'How come we hope sighs will convey a message so obnoxious we'd never say it out loud?')

Ahead the lights are red. This time I let loose an almost imperceptible snort. So imperceptible I may be able to deny its existence should Jocasta call me on it; but perceptible enough so she'll be sure to hear it.

Perfect.

I've reached the stage in the argument where I'm in pretty deep. Either I find a way of escalating this thing, or I might be forced to admit I'm being a petulant pillock. I decide to escalate it.

'It's like your thing about King Street,' I say. 'You drive all over Sydney just to avoid it. What's your problem?'

Jocasta tells me not to even *talk* to her about King Street, and says that my use of King Street to go west, when if you look at a map it actually goes south, is further proof of my galloping insanity. She then starts using the windscreen to draw various maps of Sydney, pointing out where we live ('Here,' she says, stabbing the windscreen), and how all my preferred ways home ('There, there and there') lead in virtually the opposite direction.

Then she sighs.

It's a long, bleak sigh, slipping from her lips with a mixture of exhaustion and self-pity. As best I can decode it, it contains within it the narrative of how, twenty years ago, an intelligent young woman with options in life made a series of decisions which led her, in middle-age, to be driving at 30 kilometres an hour over the Anzac Bridge with a moron.

I realise this seems a lot of information to convey in a single sigh, but you should have been there to hear its length and gurgling depth.

I permit myself a secretive smile. She's now behaving as badly as me. I think that's some sort of victory.

Despite all my efforts, we get home in record time. She says nothing. But she does smile.

I turn to her. 'That smile,' I say, decoding its message, 'that's an I-told-you-so smile, isn't it?'

49

'No,' she says archly, 'just happy to be home.'

We're in the driveway. But still, I think, some way short of being home, in any full sense of the word. Next time, I need some better directions.

Rules of Engagement

Forget the Federal Government's talk of free 'marriage training'; we need a new marriage contract — one which confronts the real compromises of married life. Before you marry, simply take this list to your proposed bloke, and see how many clauses he'll sign up for.

If he ticks less than twenty items — well, frankly, I wouldn't bother.

❑ I agree to flirt only with women of a similar body shape to that of my partner, and certainly never with anyone thinner.

❑ I agree to marvel when my partner has a whole dinner-table full of people laughing at one of her stories, even though I may have heard it once or twice before.

❑ I agree not to call our child any unusual or modish names.

❑ I agree not to cough, sneeze, breathe or otherwise suggest my own existence, during the broadcast of the medical drama *ER*.

- ❏ I agree never to drive around on a sixteenth of a tank of petrol, as I know this causes my partner anxiety.
- ❏ We will agree to disagree on the subject of my schoolmate Tony, but I will personally pay for any damage to fixtures and fittings consequent to his visits.
- ❏ I agree never, under any circumstances, to use the word 'hysterical'.
- ❏ I agree to listen, without comment, to her favourite wailing singer–songwriters.
- ❏ I agree not to give constant map directions when my partner is driving, acknowledging that, when I'm not present, she somehow manages to get around.
- ❏ I agree not to correct her when she sings the wrong words of songs.
- ❏ I agree never to mention the concept of pre-menstrual tension during or following arguments, whatever my suspicions of its role in the present hostilities.
- ❏ I agree to refrain from constantly pulling her back from street corners in the belief she was about to step in front of a passing car, acknowledging that, when I'm not present, she manages to stay alive.
- ❏ I agree, while being her partner in the card game Five Hundred, never to employ the phrase 'What sort of idiot bids eight hearts without the right bower?' even when it's true.
- ❏ I agree to sit in restaurants, and order dessert for myself, while she demurely refuses, in the full

knowledge that when it arrives, she'll polish off the lot.

❑ I agree to eschew nicknames such as 'darl', 'baby' and 'old girl'.

❑ I agree never to make separate calculations of the cost of her STD phone calls.

❑ I agree to the former on the understanding there will likewise be no adding-up of my annual credit-card spending at Theo's Liquor Mart.

❑ I agree to her use of the word 'we' when describing to her sister the back-breaking labour that I have just completed on my own, as in the sentence: 'We rebuilt the whole of the back fence last Sunday.'

❑ I agree to learn all her strange family expressions, and teach them to our children, so that these peculiar traditions may be carried on.

❑ I agree to watch as she tries on five different black tops, all seemingly identical, before enthusiastically endorsing her conviction that 'the second one is the best'.

❑ I shall remain able, however, to sense subtle changes in the wind, and adopt a sudden preference for Black Top Number Four should she change her mind.

❑ I agree, when we are old and grey, not to dye my hair before she does.

❑ I agree not to recruit her friends to my side of things during any bitter interior-decorating feuds.

❑ I agree to be sympathetic when she's sick, and not secretly imply it must be her fault.

- I agree, when I've talked about my own day at work for two and a half hours, I might occasionally remember to ask about hers.
- I agree my mid-life crisis, when it comes, will not involve a sports car, sky-diving, or guitar lessons.
- I agree to refrain from employing, at the end of arguments, any of the popular variants of 'sorry' — the barely audible sorry, the screamed sorry, or, worst of all, the conditional sorry ('I'm sorry if *you* took it that way').
- I agree male housework extends further than 'jobs involving a ladder'.
- I agree to stand adoringly in the background when she's in the limelight, and to enjoy it.
- I agree never, even in the heat of argument, to employ the remark: 'You're growing more like your mother every day.'
- I make the above agreement subject to her eschewing the observation: 'Geez, you're like your father.'
- I agree to respond to each and every one of her haircuts, over the next sixty years, as if it's a revelation, a triumph, and a sensation.
- And, finally and crucially, I agree to find her gorgeous and sexy even when she's dressed in Ugh boots and trackie daks.

The Der-Title

Film and TV critics are always calling for more subtlety and complexity on film and television. Not me. I'm already having enough trouble understanding what's going on. Plots in which people dress up as someone else. Plots involving a double-double-*double* cross. Whodunits filmed in such gloomy light that I'm still trying to work out who was murdered.

Jocasta is a patient woman. At the end of each scene, she pauses the video and explains what has happened. Usually I've got a question, something like: 'Why did her husband murder her, anyway — they seemed to be getting on so well?'

At this point, Jocasta usually lets loose a groan. But she gives me an answer: 'Well, that bloke with the black hair and the gun, he wasn't her husband, he was just a robber. The husband is this guy here.'

Then she'll start the video again and point out what appears to me to be an identical guy. Both are good-looking, tall, dark-haired. How am I meant to pick the difference?

What I need is a movie producer who'll help out the audience a little — who'll cast someone with black hair as the husband and a short blond bloke as the murderer. Or better, put one in a kilt and the other in a beard.

I don't know about you, but when I'm watching videos I never bother with the characters' names. I just form a mental picture. I think: 'Hey, there's Kilt Guy. And — oh! — he's getting out a gun. Oh no! He's murdering Beard Man.'

Of course, I know the problem with this. Take it to its furthest extent and you end up with the *Pokémon Movie*, with each character dressed head to toe in his or her own distinctive colour.

Which is exactly what I'd like to see more often in mainstream films. Just imagine *Being John Malkovich* with John Cusack in the full purple body stocking, and Cameron Diaz in the all-over Pikachu-yellow. Even I might have been able to understand what was going on.

It's even tougher when we go out to the movies, because Jocasta won't stand for any talking. All questions have to be saved until the end, so I usually just sit there, letting the movie wash over me. Years ago we went to *The French Lieutenant's Woman* which, you may remember, featured a 19th-century romance alongside a modern love story between the actors. This, naturally, was far too much for me. And for the middle-aged couple behind us.

Throughout the movie came the couple's furtive whispering: 'Why does he have a moustache? He didn't have a moustache in the last scene. Why is she wearing a miniskirt? And what is that car doing there?'

And then with a dismissive snort: 'They didn't even have cars in those days.'

Finally Jocasta had enough, swivelled in her seat and gave it to them: 'Look, there are two time scales here.

One bit's 1867, the other's now, and we're cutting from one to another. Geddit?'

Naturally I sympathised with her annoyance (while being quietly grateful for the tip-off about the plot).

The Australian Opera a few years ago introduced a form of sub-titles, flashed on a screen above the stage, for those baffled by the foreign words. They are called sur-titles. Which gave me the idea of introducing some der-titles. With der-titles, a simple message would flash on the cinema screen for all those of us who are experiencing trouble. Just like a friendly word of advice from a caring, more intelligent friend.

Imagine one of those confusing wedding scenes; the der-title would flash up at just the right moment: 'She's not marrying her brother, they just both happen to have black hair.'

Or during the climactic shoot-out: 'The guy who just shot him, he's the police officer you saw before.'

I've even started compiling some of the great der-titles of the modern cinema, to be flashed up at that crucial, confusing moment. Der-titles such as:

'Yes, she's actually a man!' — *The Crying Game*.

'The time scale is flipping backwards and forwards' — *Pulp Fiction*.

'The wife did it' — *Presumed Innocent*.

'Faye Dunaway is the girl's sister as well as the girl's mother' — *Chinatown*.

'He's repeating the same day over and over' — *Groundhog Day*.

'He's just dressing up as his mother, she's already dead' — *Psycho*.

57

'Rosebud was his sled when he was a kid' — *Citizen Kane*.

Meanwhile, back at home, Jocasta still sits, a look of resignation on her face, hitting the pause button and stoically explaining the finer points to The Space Cadet. 'What you've got to understand,' she says, 'is that Clark Kent *is* Superman.'

And then a worried glance at me. 'You shouldn't feel too bad if you didn't understand either,' she says, searching for a phrase to put me at my ease. 'It fooled Lois.'

Bring on the der-titles now and give one man back his dignity.

Being 7

There's a magic about The Space Cadet's shoelaces. However many times you tie them up, when you next look down they are loose. What is the force that drives them apart? Why do they yearn to be free? At the start of the soccer game, I tie the laces once, then thread them beneath the boot, and tie them again on top. Just to be sure, I throw in a few more grannys and a couple of bows.

It's like Houdini in the underwater packing case. Short of a length of chain and a padlock, I can do no more.

The Space Cadet runs onto the field, kicks a single ball, and the ref blows his whistle. The game is halted. His white laces flip and flop across the ground like a pair of dying seagulls.

If being seven years old was a job, with job descriptions and performance targets, The Space Cadet would meet all criteria. He is *extremely* seven.

What are the warning signs that a seven-year-old is in your presence? Here are just some of them.

1. Band-Aids represent the pinnacle of medical science. They can cure anything, especially if applied with the right amount of drama,

concern, and spotlit focus on the injured party. Best of all, they combine, in one neat package, both a medicinal device and a badge of courage — simultaneously keeping out germs while alerting the wider world to the enormous pain you've suffered. On the evidence of seven-year-olds, the medical world should already be trialing the Band-Aid for use in the battle against typhoid, Alzheimer's and leprosy.

2. Shoes belonging to a seven-year-old are always impossible to find. Removed at a whim, they then burrow into hiding — beneath the couch, behind the washing machine, underneath the grandmother. Many are never found, presumably having made a break for freedom. I wouldn't be at all surprised to come across three dozen pairs of them, all hiding-out in the roof cavity, dreaming of escape, having sly-grog parties, and building themselves a hang-glider.

3. Brushing teeth, according to a seven-year-old boy, involves waving a toothbrush towards your mouth, and inhaling the faint smell of spearmint. Similarly, washing hands involves throwing a wary glance towards the soap-dish before making a dash for the backyard. Just as having a wee involves walking into a bathroom, and spotting the existence of a toilet in the vague direction that you're aiming. 'The toilet and I were in the same room at the same time. What more do you expect?'

4. Just as the shoelaces seem to spring apart, so does the seven-year-old head repel all head-gear. A hat,

placed firmly on the head as you leave the house, will have vanished by the time you've reached the car. Hence my campaign to reinstate the bonnet, complete with a hearty chin-strap. Psychological damage for a whole generation of seven-year-old boys? Sure. But at least it's sun-safe.

5. The list of acceptable sandwich fillings declines every day by one ingredient. Until there's nothing left but peanut butter.

6. Discussing and debating the rules of a game always takes longer than actually playing it. It's like watching the middle management of a very inefficient firm. No-one ever actually does anything, but there's much *appearance* of activity.

7. What's with the whole stick thing? The Space Cadet collects them wherever he goes. He walks around with them stuffed in his pockets or slid into his belt. Some are imagined swords and guns, but many are just sticks. 'You haven't dropped my stick?' he'll ask, eyes awash with panic. And so we march back into the bush, stepping over three million sticks, in order to find The Stick.

8. The pain of an injury depends on the circumstances of its occurrence. The average seven-year-old, while showing off on the trampoline for his glamorous sixteen-year-old baby-sitter, can plunge headfirst into a metal post and come up smiling. 'It was nothing', he'll say, brushing the trickle of blood away from his eyes, and staggering slightly. But try brushing his hair ...

9. In his own bed he'll sleep curled up in the corner, looking angelic. Allow him into yours, and he'll sprawl on an exact diagonal, arms and legs thrown out in a frozen star-jump. How can somebody who's just over a metre tall, and thin as a post, entirely fill a queen-size bed? These are the mysteries of being seven.

10. At birthday and Christmas times he will open the most obscure gift — a three-metre blow-up duck; a matchstick model of the National Gallery; a complete kit for the preparation of a Japanese banquet — and say, instantly and sincerely: 'This is *exactly* what I needed.'

11. There are as many excuses for getting out of bed as there are minutes between Bedtime at 9.00 p.m. and Final Unconsciousness at 10.00 p.m. Need for water, ghosts, need for more water, noises outside, blanket too hot, need for third glass of water, blanket too cold, pillow too lumpy, and — yes — the need to go to the toilet five times, due to over-consumption of water.

12. With every day, a new enthusiasm, and never the same two days running. A paddle-pop-stick castle, a clay pot, a garden that's his very own, a Lego-and-dead-grass tableau, and a cubby for a pet frog should he ever get one. If only some of the enthusiasms lasted two days, the house might not be so full of just-started castles, pots, gardens, tableaux and cubbies. But, by then, his laces will stay tied. And he won't be seven.

Girls' Jeans

The younger shop assistant in Jay Jay's Jeans was eyeing me over, assessing whether I was man enough to cop her rather rash proposal. But something must have clicked right with her: maybe the way I was standing, maybe the shape of my bum in the pair of Levi's 501s.

'You could buy that pair,' she said, 'but we've got exactly the same thing for about $60 less.'

'Exactly the same?'

'Well, exactly the same except they are *girls*' jeans.'

Instantly, I felt myself flush: I'd spent a lifetime trying to get into girls' pants. The girls' Levi's were $33; the boys' $99. I was presented with a stark choice between my identity as a man — the whole history of male achievement on this planet — and saving $66. Naturally, I went for the dollars.

There are times in every man's life when he's tempted to wear women's clothing, and this was mine. I went into the changing room and slipped on the pants; they were cut a little differently, but who would notice? And they were a *lot* cheaper.

I walked out and modelled the pants. Both shop assistants approved.

'Actually, I think they look better on you than the men's,' said the younger one, with what I felt was unnecessary enthusiasm.

'Yes,' said the other, '*some* men just suit the girls' cut.'

I knew exactly what sort of men she meant. Those with child-bearing hips.

I met Jocasta and the kids back at the car, and, still a little embarrassed, still a little hesitant, whispered all about it into my beloved's ear, all about the money, and the cut, and what they said about the pants' suiting me.

And, of course, Jocasta reacted with her usual demure sensitivity. 'Hah!' she yahooed to the kids, slapping her thigh. 'Look at your father, he's wearing girls' pants!'

I wonder whether you happen to have a pre-teen boy in your family. Because only then might you understand exactly how funny such a child might find the idea of his father wearing girls' pants. And the answer is very, very, very funny indeed.

So there we were in the car. Me sitting in my cheap girls' jeans; Jocasta trying so hard not to laugh that she's spluttering over the windscreen; and Batboy paralytic in the back seat, red in the face, panting to get the air in, chanting: 'Girls' pants, girls' pants.'

But Batboy is a comedian, and he knows there's nothing like good timing. So he calms down and waits; waits for that moment back at home when we pass in the corridor, and he looks up and delivers his cheery greeting: 'Hello, *girl*.'

By now it's clear: I should have stopped experimenting with wearing women's clothing when I was sixteen, like all my mates. Whatever the saving, the jeans are cursed.

On Sunday I wear them to a barbecue. Within minutes Jocasta has told everyone, and all the women demand to know what size I take in women's jeans. So I tell them the size, and no longer am I taunted for wearing 'girls' jeans'; I'm taunted for wearing '*fat* girls' jeans'.

On Monday, I wear them to work — knowing I have to take The Space Cadet to school on the bus, and so jeans will be good. But can I shake off the Curse Of The Plump Girls' Jeans?

We're on the bus for ten minutes, when The Space Cadet works loose the top of his drink bottle. Gracefully, he pours the juice onto my crotch. No longer do I look like a plump girl riding on the bus; now I look like a plump girl with a bladder-control problem riding on the bus.

The stain looks shocking, a big dark patch spreading from my beltline to halfway down my thighs, and yet, at the school gate, no-one takes any notice. The other parents have seen Juice-Bottle Lap before, just as they have seen Vegemite Collar, Peanut-Butter Shoulders and Weet-Bix Bum.

But at work, people are staring. First up, I have a message to see the boss, so I'm standing in his office in my girls' jeans, holding a copy of *The Bulletin* over my crotch, and we are discussing my responsibilities. And I can see he's eyeing my soaking crotch, thinking: 'Who'd let him control anything, when he can't control his own urinary tract.'

Finally the jeans dry. I pick up The Space Cadet from after-school care and stumble home, to see my family, standing there at the front door, a picture of warmth.

'Hello, girl,' says Batboy, with a big, toothy smile.

'Hello, girl,' says Jocasta, with a kiss.

The girl is home.

3

Jocasta decides that our discussion of my
drinking problem needs one more element.
It needs Simon to be involved. Now, Simon is
a good bloke ... but he's also a doctor.

The Girl Magnet

The way my parents brought me up has left me with many advantages in life, chief of which is a watertight excuse should I ever snap and become a crazed psychopath. The reasons are too numerous to mention, at least until the judge calls for the submissions on sentencing. But we could start with my childhood wallpaper.

While most parents decorate their eight-year-old's room by buying four litres of baby-blue paint and a night lamp, mine decided the room should also have a 'feature wall'. This involved James Bond wallpaper, complete with a recurring pattern made up of a sports car, a glinting revolver, some quite realistic bullet-holes and a group of semi-naked women — presumably evil Soviet spies.

In terms of my own psychosexual development, it's hard to assess the exact impact of the James Bond design, although it did lead to constant dreams in which I was brutally murdered by wallpaper. And, years later, I still find myself strangely anxious in groups, particularly those comprised of half-naked women with Russian accents.

Of course, as the 1960s gave way to the 1970s, feature walls around the country were painted over, and young minds began the slow struggle to regain their equilibrium. Which is when they brought in novelty underpants.

Novelty underpants were a sort of '70s version of the feature wall: while the rest of you would be dressed in fawn, your underpants would be covered with orange geometrics or, worse, actual cartoon characters.

Again, we can only speculate as to the deep effects on my developing mind, knowing that deep beneath my school uniform, Barney Rubble and Fred Flintstone were playing inside my pants. And — just maybe — protecting me from the next attack of the half-naked Russians.

It was a strange idea, really, the personality jockette, and most men just settled for the Jockette of the Month, which offered twelve new designs each year — a marketing idea which collapsed after it emerged that most men thought you were meant to wear the single pair all month.

The exotically patterned jockette survived, however, and quickly built a reputation among teenage boys as a real Girl Magnet — with considerable effort being expended, before each date, choosing which one to wear.

No women, you understand, actually got to see the pattern — at least, not the patterns worn by the sexual no-hopers in my peer group. We must have believed the girls could just tell — that somehow they'd know that beneath our jeans there lurked a pair of red ones. And that, given the subconscious rays being radiated by these, our lucky undies, the girls would be rendered helpless.

'Hey, Liz, look at Richard over there — there's just something about him that makes me think, I don't know ... red.'

'Yeah, Hanna, I know what you mean — suddenly I know it's right for me to have his baby.'

Later in life, we'd discover that a 'pair of luckies' was essential to all sorts of events, and not just adolescent dating, including:

(a) the pay-rise 'lucky undie';
(b) the public speech 'lucky undie'; and
(c) the university exam 'lucky undie'.

Yet unanswered questions crowd in: if a bloke's lucky colour is red — and it always seems to be — why doesn't he just buy two dozen reds, so he can always be encased in a pair of luckies? The answer being (hushed voice): *'Because they would lose their power, that's why.'* The lucky undie is a delicate instrument — and must be left to accumulate its power in the drawer, only to emerge when needed; when its power can be suddenly unleashed on the unsuspecting.

And, of course, it's not only about colour. It's also about fit — a subtle matter that cannot be bought in bulk, but has to be chanced upon in that perfect pair that's not too loose, and not too tight; the one with the action gusset and the nurturing support.

Yet despite it all, the magic undies never quite worked and we were forced into desperate experimentation with other suspected Girl Magnets — conducting dangerous trials with devices such as the polyester body-shirt, the shoulder-length hair and even the Janis Ian record collection.

These were the early days in the development of the Girl Magnet. There were many in our brave experimental team who never recovered after these devices went tragically wrong in the field — young men who made the fatal error of smelling their own armpits after wearing a body-shirt, and those, both male and female, exposed to what we now realise were near-lethal levels of Janis Ian.

If only, years back, when I was eight years old, I'd had the guts to stand up to my parents and quote the words which Oscar Wilde uttered on his death bed: 'Either this wallpaper goes, or I do.'

Simon Says

'If you drank less you might look a bit more like Simon.' Jocasta makes the statement baldly, factually, letting it drop on the mat between us. Simon, who has invited us to stay the weekend, is next door, in the kitchen, mixing up some muesli and singing chirpily. Every time he hits the high note it's like a knife into my hangover.

Simon is my oldest friend. We've been mates since we were twelve. And old schoolmates are important to a man. They are great for telling stories, for laughing about old times, for sharing a few confidences. They are less useful, however, when your partner starts using them as a point of comparison in order to describe the extent of your own physical decline.

'Simon looks just *so* good,' says Jocasta, warming to her theme. 'Well, actually he looks *great*. Such a fresh face. And so happy in the mornings.'

Next door, Simon hits a particularly high note in his rendition of 'Morning Has Broken', causing some sort of electrical storm in the nerve endings of my brain.

'I mean, look at him,' says Jocasta, waving airily towards the kitchen as if Simon's beauty was of such staggering intensity as to be easily appreciated through a double-brick wall. 'He doesn't wake up looking haggard. He doesn't wake up feeling tired. And that's because he's sensible about his drinking.'

I let loose a groan. I am under attack, and just when all verbal skills — all the skills of counter-attack — have been momentarily disarmed by alcohol abuse.

It can't get worse than this, I think. But it does.

Jocasta decides that our discussion of my drinking problem needs one more element. It needs Simon to be involved. Now, Simon is a good bloke, and it's been lovely to visit him over the holidays, and to learn his recipe for a really sustaining muesli. But he's also a doctor.

And so when Jocasta marches us both into the kitchen and asks Simon whether he thinks his old friend is drinking too much, he says: 'Yes, I think he definitely needs to cut down.' He pauses, stirring in another handful of organic bran: 'Four standard drinks a day is about the limit. Plus, of course, two alcohol-free days each week.'

He throws in a handful of apricot chunks, before continuing breezily: 'Although, of course, there may already be some permanent brain damage.'

This is the problem of having a friend who ends up a doctor. One minute you're both fifteen years old and getting smashed together on Smirnoff hip flasks while stealing your parents' cars. The next minute you're both turning forty and he's giving you a lecture. Usually on the state of your prostate.

Jocasta, of course, seizes her moment of triumph. 'Let's see you do it, right now, in front of Simon. Admit you're drinking too much.'

For a moment I consider doing just that, before pulling myself together. Admitting it would be against the Marital Code of Arguments, the very first clause of which is Never Admit Anything. (As in the comment: 'I was not drunk; it was just that your sister's cooking upset the delicate balance of my stomach.')

What's crucial is to not let the mere facts of the case get in the way of victory. Especially since — under the Marital Code of Arguments — both parties should feel free to range over contentious issues from the distant past. (As in the comment: 'I may drink too much, but at least I know how to reverse-park without running over the neighbour's cat.')

Yet this morning Jocasta isn't playing by the rules. She isn't point-scoring. She isn't shouting. She isn't even bothering to claim that, back in 1979, it was the cat's fault. Instead she is adopting the most frightening tone of all: the (gulp) tone of sympathetic concern.

'You'll develop brain damage,' says Jocasta, her eyes soft and sad, 'and then I'll have to live with you ... watching as you go into a decline. It will be so tragic.'

I drink a *smidgin* more than Simon, and already Jocasta's mind has fast-forwarded through the whole florid plot line. 'You'll go vague, and then get this big veiny red nose, and start smelling of whisky before breakfast.'

Here Jocasta's voice started to break up as she moved relentlessly through my later years — the alcoholic seizures, the grim faces of the doctors, the decision to move me out of home — and then the sad scene, as Batboy and The Space Cadet are brought to visit me in the Sea-View Guesthouse, walking up into the bunkhouse where I am staying with the other men, all of us with our little metal beds, padding down the hallway from the shower wrapped in our scratchy little towels.

'I'll try to remember you as you were before it all went so terribly wrong,' Jocasta sobs.

Even Simon, busy in the corner polishing his muesli container, is starting to get pretty choked up.

I knew the time had come. For once, I was going to have to break the Sacred Oath of the Marital Argument. I was going to have to Admit Blame.

And so this morning I have promised to improve. *Anything* to escape Jocasta's powers of description.

More Waist, Less Speed

We all know that turning forty poses its own challenges. But, when my turn comes, I don't need a birth certificate to confirm the event. In the weeks leading up to this, I've already clocked up forty reasons to know I've turned forty.

1. I find myself no longer thinking about sex all the time, only once every 12.7 seconds.
2. I start buying Lite White.
3. When choosing a film, I base the decision not on the director, the star, or the writer, but on which cinema has the most comfortable seats.
4. For the first time since I was five years old, my age and my pants size have become alarmingly similar.
5. Forget the policemen looking young. That new spokeswoman for the Combined Pensioners Association looks like a real goer.
6. I catch myself using the phrase, 'young people today'.

7. I see a friend's garden and discover, as if by magic, that I have The Knowledge: the hedge on the left is Box; on the right, Murraya.

8. Passing thought: 'That Malcolm Fraser seems a reasonable person.'

9. I have a long discussion with friends about their kitchen benchtops.

10. I make the change to Lite Cheese.

11. I ring a company and order a kitchen-benchtop pamphlet.

12. I notice that the music on the easy-listening radio station has suddenly improved, and they're now playing what I judge to be 'really up-to-date music'.

13. So are the Musak people.

14. I start buying Lite Biscuits.

15. I stop tucking in my shirts, letting them hang out, in the hope that someone might mistake The Belly for a chance billow of fabric. I realise this is but one short step from the Kaftan.

16. The pamphlet on benchtops arrives and I take it to bed instead of a novel.

17. I start buying Lite Ham.

18. I discover I have finally forgotten everything I learnt at school, except for the adiabatic lapse rate (3.3 degrees per 1 000 feet) and the fact that guys with red hair make dirty fighters.

19. I realise, in the last month, I've painted four separate items in Brunswick Green.

20. I discover the insolent youngster hanging around the doctor's surgery is in fact the doctor.

21. And he wants to do *what*?
22. I buy a book about garden compost.
23. Passing thought: 'I must get a file together so I can keep warranties and receipts all in one place.'
24. I get inordinately upset if I miss the start of the 7.00 a.m. radio news, as if national security is dependent on my being completely briefed on public affairs.
25. I find myself becoming deeply annoyed when someone uses 'disinterested' when they mean 'uninterested'.
26. Batboy beats me at tennis.
27. I approach heavy lifting around the house with a sense not of how much I have to prove, but how much I have to lose.
28. Batboy beats me at running.
29. I become more patient. And, occasionally, a patient.
30. The thing we have in a joint is no longer called 'marijuana'. It's called arthritis.
31. I start buying Lite Ice Cream.
32. I am alarmed to discover that someone's decided to print the instructions on the Panadol bottle in increasingly smaller type-sizes.
33. The benchtop company rings and I choose the second-cheapest product, rather than the cheapest.
34. I preface political arguments by saying 'I think there's a lot of truth in what you're saying', and actually mean it.
35. I buy Lite Jam.

36. A single game of soccer leaves me unable to walk until at least the next World Cup.
37. For the first time, my annual dentistry bill exceeds my combined spending on clothes and CDs.
38. I describe a sixty-year-old friend as 'middle-aged'.
39. The benchtops arrive, together with a 'care' booklet. I take it to bed to read, but fall asleep during the first page.
40. I consider having a Saturday night birthday bash, but realise this may involve missing *The Bill*. Apparently, tonight the boss has a terrible argument with DCI Jack Meadows!

The Fairyland
Frontline

We're at the Clown and Fairy Party Centre and things are about to turn nasty. The mother of the birthday girl is standing at the counter, holding her receipt threateningly, a steely look on her face. 'Exactly how,' she asks the man behind the counter, 'could you lose the booking?'

The receipt certainly shows a booking has been made. For precisely this time. And for a full fairy party ('Cake, stories and games — all with a real fairy! Just drop off the kids — and we'll do the rest!!').

Furthermore, the receipt, which the mother is now waving with a series of angry jerking motions, shows the party will be attended by fifteen girls and one boy.

That one boy is The Space Cadet, who now stands close to my side, his suspicions growing, as the room fills with little girl fairies, each of them wearing their own body-weight in tulle.

The Space Cadet, by contrast, is wearing his best outfit — blue check lumberjack shirt, navy blue 'kerchief, black cowboy boots, and hair gelled up to resemble that of his favourite singer, Elvis. In the sea of pink tulle, he certainly stands out.

Suddenly, there's a surge of fairies towards the locked door of the fairy cave, and a bit of shoving. The sparkly wings are tangling and bending; the tulle compressing like a coiled spring. If all of them breathe out at once, some fairies may well fly.

With the party delayed, the mood among the fairies is darkening. I fear it can't be long before the wands come out. A tremble of fear runs through The Space Cadet's small body.

Back at the counter, the manager is still trying to explain how he lost the booking. Foolishly, he attempts the truculent response. 'Look, lady,' he says to my friend, the mother of the birthday girl, and momentarily I feel sorry for him. The last guy to say 'Look, lady' to Diana is now successfully employed as Chief Eunuch to the Sultan of Dubai.

Oblivious, he stumbles on: 'What am I meant to do? Even if I admit I've stuffed up, how can I suddenly come up with a bloody fairy? At 10.00 a.m. on a Sunday!'

He gives a little wink, and attempts a sort of greasy, unctuous smile. 'I mean, lady, I can't just wave a magic wand.'

The manager of the Clown and Fairy Party Centre may well believe that humour is the best way to diffuse a threatening situation. Isn't it amazing just how wrong a bloke can be.

Fresh waves of fairies are now entering the shop, part of a second party which, it emerges, this bloke's also forgotten to book. There are now thirty-six fairies packed into the corridor in front of the fairy's magic cave — all of them covered in tulle, their sparkly garlands aquiver.

Thirty-six girls, plus The Space Cadet, who's now sitting sullenly on a polystyrene toadstool, glancing occasionally towards me — his big eyes full of reproach. The question 'How could you do this to me?' springs to mind.

There are now two enraged mothers at the counter. And a manager whose eyes are full of fear. He might not be able to find a fairy in a hurry, but he's facing a terrifying oversupply of ogres.

'Look, pal,' says my friend, stabbing her receipt towards the manager's face, 'you find a fairy, a real magic fairy, and find one fast.'

'Otherwise,' chimes in the other mother, producing her daughter's large, spiked wand. 'I'm sure I could make *this* disappear.'

A tremor passes across the manager's face. 'Well,' he concedes, with some uncertainty, 'I suppose we could ring Tracey.'

It takes an hour for Tracey to appear — an hour in which the thirty-six little girl fairies work their own vengeful magic on the Clown and Fairy Party Centre, while The Space Cadet sensibly creeps ever lower behind his toadstool.

But finally Tracey makes it — and in so doing makes it abundantly clear why she's not her manager's first option. The night before, it appears, Tracey has been making magic in her own special way. As fairies go, she's had a pretty big night, with — from the look of things — liberal supplies of fairy dust.

'Ahhh, g'day kids,' says Trace, her eyes a most magical shade of red. The little girls look up, full of innocent hope, but Trace's bleary eyes instead settle on The Space Cadet, the cloud of confusion suddenly clearing from her mind.

'Bugger me, it's Elvis. Hey, come here, pal.'

And so The Space Cadet slips off his magic toadstool, and comes to sit on Trace's lap, there to luxuriate in her confusion. And to enjoy that morning's *particularly* wild fairy stories.

As fairy parties go, it was one of the best.

Old-Man Emu

The Space Cadet, as always, has a teenage girl at his beck and call: he is sitting on our young friend's shoulders, being carried down to the beach. I'm on the other side of the road, walking with Batboy and Jocasta, and I can't stop myself saying something. Putting on a bad southern American accent, I yell across the road: 'You know you'll spoil that boy — spoil him rotten.'

The only problem: just as I yell it out, a car is slowly motoring past. A woman is driving. There's a child in the back. Her window is open. She thinks I'm talking to her.

Coming to a halt, and genuinely baffled, she says: 'I'm sorry, what did you say?' I stammer an excuse. I was just talking to my friend. The one, um, over there.

By now, though, there is no-one over there. The lady shakes her head, saddened by the proliferation of insane people since community housing policies were introduced. And then she drives off. Which is when I notice Batboy, standing by my side. He is rigid with embarrassment.

He's stock still, staring intently at the ground, and has swivelled his shoulders away from me. His body language says it all: 'I'm just waiting here to cross the road. The loud fat man? Never seen him before in my life.'

Of course, every child thinks they've got the world's most embarrassing father. But Batboy's sure of it.

Eventually he glances up and tells me what he thinks. 'Oh, Dad,' he says, but the 'dad' is somewhat elongated. 'Daaaaaaaaaaaad.' It sounds half-way between a simple reproach and the sort of keening you might get at an African funeral.

The reason we're going to the beach is to see an Aboriginal dance troupe who are performing on the sand. And, guess what? Halfway through their act they call for volunteers from the audience. Ever game, I struggle to my feet. And as I do, I notice Batboy's face. He is agog. He cannot believe it. *Twice* in one day.

This time he almost weeps it. 'Oh, Daaaaaaaad.'

As it happens, the Aboriginal dancers only get two responses to their kind request for volunteers. There's me. And a three-year-old boy.

We are being taught to do the Emu dance, which involves parading around the beach wobbling our bottoms, and occasionally pecking at the sand. After we've pecked, we're also meant to do this little wiggle to signify the seed passing down the Emu's long throat — an action which, I must say, I perform with some considerable flamboyance. As does the three-year-old.

By the time I'm finished, Batboy has his hands over his eyes. Jocasta is saying to him: 'Just relax. No-one knows it's your father. We'll pretend we just happen to be sitting here.'

They are both angled away, pretending to look elsewhere. I realise there's something about this reaction

86

that I quite like. Finally I figure it: suddenly I feel so wonderfully eccentric. Here I am: a mortgage man with greying temples, yet through the baffled eyes of my son I remain one of the most bizarre and unconventional people in the land.

Here is the wonderful egalitarianism of it: to each of our children, we are it. The bee's knees. The ultimate. Each of us gets the award: The World's *Most* Embarrassing Parent.

A habit of singing when walking past the school gates. An old car which belches on its way to the shops. A tendency to wear home-made drawstring pants to the end-of-year-concert. Not big things. But enough, when viewed through our children's humiliated eyes, to turn each of us into the Che Guevara of the Suburbs.

We go home. Sunday night. Homework to be done. And Batboy's not keen.

'Do your homework, or else.'

'Or else, what,' he says.

Suddenly the idea strikes. 'The Emu dance. I think your friends might like to see it. Especially the wiggle when I swallow the seed.'

He smiles, knowing I'm joking, and then looks at me again. He *thinks* I'm joking. But maybe he'll do his homework anyway. When you're son to the world's absolutely, incontrovertibly *most* embarrassing parent, you can never be too cautious.

Holiday Laws

Every summer, whether you head inland or up the coast, some things seem to stay the same. Here are just some of the strange laws of holiday life.

1. The Bowling Club Restaurant is Always Chinese. What's the story? What exactly is the connection between the game of lawn bowls and the cuisine of southern China? Why not a Thai or Indian place? Why not a cook-your-own-steak joint? And exactly when did the secretary–managers of Australia sign the secret deal that would condemn their members and guests to an unrelieved diet of sweet and sour pork?

2. The Manager of the Local Council Pool is Always a Complete Bastard. Give a man a loudspeaker system, a whistle, and long-term exposure to hundreds of small children, and what do you expect? Although we must admit it: the more fascist the manager, the cleaner and more sparkling his pool.

3. The Local Butcher is Always Friendly and Funny. Big town, small town, coast or inland. Who

knows the reason? Is it the hormones in the beef? Or that only he knows how much meat extender is going into his sausages?

4. There is No Town in Australia Which Does Not Claim to be Annual Winner of the National Tidy Town Competition. And virtually no pub which isn't 'historic'.

5. Thirty Per Cent of Any Summer Holiday Is Spent Trying to Find the Sun-screen. By all means, take ten tubes. Fill the boot with them. By Day Two they will all be missing. Ditto toothbrushes. Favourite Bears. The car keys.

6. The Size of the Motel Pool is in Inverse Proportion to the Size of the Sign Advertising the Pool. Just as: the size of the helpings in the motel restaurant is in inverse proportion to the number of descriptive adjectives on the menu.

7. The Tarmac Gives Over to Dirt Just After You've Passed the Property of the Local Mayor.

8. Every town must have a claim to fame. There are two Gateways to the Warrumbungles, three Sweet Corn Capitals of Australia, ten Homes to the State's Tallest Tree, and — way out west, over the great artesian basin — we even visited the Home of the World's Largest Bore. What we need is a new generation of signs: 'Welcome to Ordinarytown — Home to the State's Most Spurious Claim.'

9. The tent will never go back into the tent bag. The milk always falls over in the Esky. There's a rock under each tent peg. There's a natural watercourse beneath your sleeping bag. Etc., etc.

10. The Availability of Fish Decreases as You Get Closer to the Coast. We bought terrific fresh flathead in Tamworth, and then spent a week by the sea eating beef hamburgers (presumably trucked in from the Western Plains). Who needs to be well-travelled when your food is?

11. The Dirtier the Truck Stop, the Better the Hamburgers.

12. The More Poetic the Name of the Town, the More Dreary it Will Be. Every holiday we spend hours driving up side roads, intoxicated by the allure of the names on the map. Windy Glen. Sassafras. River Bend. They are always ugly. Or nonexistent. By contrast, the really beautiful joints are all called things like Coalmine or Abattoirville. Consider the example of Sydney's most beautiful waterway: Pittwater. Why don't they just call it Cesspit and be done with it?

13. The Map Makers of Inland Australia Have a Rich Fantasy Life. Towns with big dots on the map that don't exist. Large rivers, traced in blue, that haven't flowed for decades. Tourist Attractions which last attracted someone in the late 1950s.

14. The More Distant the Beach, the More Likely You Are to Find Your Towel or Caravan Parked Next to Someone You Know. In my case: my boss. Frankly, I was hoping to keep the sight of my new pink rash-vest between me and my family. 'Just one picture, for the staff notice-board,' she said, producing the camera.

Back to Work

When you get back to work after holidays, you realise it's all wrong. The whole set-up. Who thought up these rules? Who decided we had time for this 'work' thing? During holidays the body forgets about these indignities; the soul stretches its wings. Now the harness is back on. With every rut in the road, the cart pulls hard against the now-softened skin. You realise: this *hurts*.

For instance:

6.30 a.m. The alarm clock goes off. This cannot be right. I feel *terrible*. An army of pixies is stabbing tiny spears into my eyeballs. The roof of my mouth has been carpeted with a shag-pile off the walls of the local RSL.

Cleverly, I incorporate the alarm clock into my dreams. I'm in a burning building, with the fire alarm screaming. Flames begin to consume my body — my hair is on fire and my testicles explode. This is extremely painful, but still better than waking up.

6.40 a.m. The back-up alarm goes off. I roll out of bed and try to focus. The day ahead involves no swimming, no tennis, and no sitting around reading novels. A few grains of sand, lying on the floor near my sandals, mock me with a rollicking laugh. Ha, ha, ha.

6.45 a.m. Reluctantly, I begin to get dressed. I can't understand who invented this gear. The dark pants and the white shirt, and then the tie — the personalised number-plate of the male worker. My body felt fine in the holiday gear — the XXL T-shirt and the board shorts. The belly swung free. The feet saluted the sun from the deck of my blue rubber thongs.

Now, I wrap the tie around my neck, and tighten it to the point where it's only vaguely uncomfortable. Perfect. It's hard not to notice how similar it is to a hangman's noose — the free end hanging down just where the boss can easily grab it. A whole army of male commuters — each with our personalised noose. Thank God, we're allowed to choose the colour, which is not the case in many other death-row situations. Mine's a zany individualist yellow. How about yours?

6.55 a.m. I eat breakfast while standing up at the sink. Between mouthfuls, enter room of older son and attempt to wake him via time-honoured method of screaming and slapping. I return to sink for further mouthful of soggy Weet-Bix, scream again at son, pack dishwasher, eat more Weet-Bix, scream at son, pack bag, then scream again at son. Two more hours of this, and at least one of us might be fully awake.

7.05 a.m. I stand at sink, and shave. What's the story? That the male must remove overt signs of his masculinity before entering the workplace? Glumly, I work the razor, convinced it's all a metaphor for castration — the male worker proving himself compliant and cowered. Thus distracted, I cut myself in five places.

8.15 a.m. I exit house, looking like Norman Gunston, and drive rapidly into nearest traffic jam. This morning it takes twenty minutes to travel one block, and another forty to reach the city.

9.15 a.m. I rush to my desk. Following a month away, I have 176 e-mail messages, nearly all concerning an air-conditioning malfunction in the Adelaide branch office. As revenge, I e-mail all Adelaide with my views on the proper disposal of nose-hairs.

10.05 a.m. My computer password has expired, and I can't remember how to use the voicemail. Solving these problems takes forty minutes. I decide to leap to my death, but discover the windows are screwed into the frames. Which can only mean that someone has tried this before.

10.45 a.m. There's a meeting with management, with much discussion of our 'mission statement'. The word 'facilitate' is also used. There must be at least one window in which the screws are loose.

1.05 p.m. I queue interminably for a sandwich, and choose something dull and calorie-controlled because 'I'm not on holidays now.'

1.30 p.m. Go back downstairs and buy three chocolate bars to lift mood, since 'I'm not on holidays now.'

2.00–6.00 p.m. I actually do some work. Make decisions. And remember holidays in which main decision was whether to have a second beer after lunch. (The sensible answer to which, by the way, is always 'No.')

6.45 p.m. I drive rapidly into traffic jam, and sit as time passes. Whole days go past getting through the inner west; governments are elected and deposed; the polar ice caps melt and refreeze.

7.30 p.m. Fall asleep. Soon the shoulders will be hardened to the harness; the body will have forgotten there's another way. My next holiday is only eleven months away.

4

'Actually, I'm pretty sick myself,' says Jocasta,
a day later, lying prone across the hallway,
and groaning. 'It's pretty close to child-birth;
I'd say eight-tenths of a child-birth. I may
need a little looking after myself.'

Cold Comfort

You'd hardly recognise Jocasta — sweeping into my room with a tray, on which was soup (the can opened by her own hand) and what she called 'toast soldiers for my sick soldier'. There was even a flower, a rather sad-looking daisy, plonked into a Vegemite glass. It was all so utterly unlike Jocasta, I started to worry. Maybe I was sicker than I thought.

A request that Jocasta should prepare soup is normally greeted by a hollow laugh, and seconds later a well-aimed copy of *The Universal Cookbook* will come flying though the air. Already, the children know the drill: after shouting out any food request to either of us, they momentarily duck.

But here was Jocasta, fussing around my bed like a nurse from a *Carry On* movie, leaning over me with health-inspiring bosoms and a kindly smile. The disease may have rendered me asthmatic and thick-headed, but it has turned Jocasta meek and sweet. Now *that's* a virus.

Truth is, most women are powerless against a pale and sickly man. It's a remarkable effect to witness, which may be why so many men, over the years, have become skilled at milking it. Some even making use of the Bambi Eyes (wide open, beseeching, injured). It's rotten that a person has to go this far to get a little sympathy. But, over time, I've found it's necessary.

My mother, for example, has always been of the view that illness is a sign of moral decay and misbehaviour. It deserves no sympathy, and certainly no treatment.

Report to her that you went to the doctor and that he said your illness is serious, and suddenly she is concerned. 'What? You went to a *doctor*?' (Incredulous pause on other end of phone.) 'Well, no wonder you're sick.'

She thinks most illness is caused by consuming over-rich food and indulging in disgusting, modern practices, such as the eating of garlic and going outdoors without germ-repelling white gloves.

In terms of parenting, she always believed her main duty was to remind me how generally lucky I was. As in the exchange:

'Mum, Mum, it's terrible, I've just fallen off my bike and gashed my leg, which is now bleeding horribly.'

'*Well, just think what a lucky boy you are to have a bike from which to fall.*'

(You'll notice: more effort placed in achieving the proper grammatical construction than in fetching a bandage to staunch the by now Amazon River-like bloodflow.)

Meanwhile, there is my doctor friend Simon — perfectly pleasant I'm sure to his own patients, but utterly unsympathetic to family and friends. One day I plan to decapitate myself in front of Simon, just to hear him look up from his newspaper and mumble: 'Oh, Richard do pull yourself together.'

So no sympathy is on offer without a bit of theatrical effort — which luckily is not beyond me. Perhaps these same performances have been spotted in your house?

The John Wayne

I'm in bed, and Jocasta has come in with some aspirin. My aim: to subtly indicate the Massive Extent of My Illness, without revealing that I'm a whinger and malingerer. I take John Wayne as my model. For instance: the moment when he gets a tomahawk through his skull, and just does one of those tight, brave smiles. The Courageous Little Smile That Masks Indescribable Pain. I flash one at Jocasta — letting it wobble a bit on my face, just to show the depth of the pain — and suddenly her brain explodes in a hormone storm. With a squawk of pity, she runs off to make more soup.

The Lord Byron

Day Two, and the Duke's losing his power. As her footsteps approach, I fall wanly backwards — and reveal 'The Lord Byron'. Pale and interesting, head lolling loosely, the eyes focused on the middle distance. Death from consumption may be rare in the inner west, but it's clearly what I've got. Jocasta runs off to starch my collars.

The Camille

Day Three, and the illness gets really bad. So bad I find myself unable to face alcohol of any sort. 'Bugger,' I think, 'I didn't know I was *that* sick.' Shaken, I return to my bed, and commence enacting the death scene from *Camille*. 'It was terrible,'

I report to Jocasta. 'I looked into the fridge, and I felt . . . I felt nothing. I wasn't *interested*.'

DIARY NOTE: 'The Camille' does not work. Expected sympathy does not eventuate. Patient greeted instead with torrent of abuse. DO NOT ATTEMPT AGAIN.

The Brando

Day Four, and I unveil 'The Brando'. Lying around unshaven in my white singlet, I yell up the hallway: 'Stella!' Finally, Jocasta responds and I give her the works: self-pity, morose introspection, shambling gait, and a complete inability to articulate simple thoughts. 'Ah,' she says brightly, 'you seem to be almost completely back to normal.'

DIARY NOTE: strategies no longer working. Jocasta has hormones back under control. Last soup came from kitchen days ago! Toast soldiers all gone! What can be done?

The Last Gasp

Notice Jocasta referring to my illness as 'the flu'. Frankly, it's an insult. I'd be better off seeing Simon. Or even my mother. What I've got is some sort of unusual virus. Probably a medical first. Doesn't she realise men never get anything as commonplace as 'the flu'? That's for women. For instance: Jocasta.

Actually, just as I'm getting better, Jocasta is coming down with something pretty similar. Only not as bad. For instance, she's not moaning or whingeing much, and is sitting quite pluckily in bed. Remarkable, isn't it, how the strain of a virus can weaken so sharply in the space of a few days.

Part of the problem, I think, is the lack of an objective pain rating that could separate the malingerers (i.e. women) from those Struggling On Despite Enormous Odds (i.e. men).

I'd like a pain thermometer: pop it under the arm, and be able to announce that I'm suffering an '8'. After all, women have this. As in the phrase: 'It was worse than childbirth.' Notice how they choose the one scale of measurement in which we can't compete — leaving themselves luxuriating on the illness highground.

'Actually, I'm pretty sick myself,' says Jocasta, a day later, lying prone across the hallway, and groaning. 'It's pretty close to childbirth; I'd say eight-tenths of a childbirth. I may need a little looking after myself.'

She looks up with beseeching Bambi Eyes, and suddenly there seems nothing for it but to pull myself together, pop her in bed, and make soup.

Luckily, that's when my mother rings.

'Can you talk to Jocasta, Mum. I think she's been eating restaurant food again and going outside without her gloves.'

Killers in the Kitchen

There's now good evidence that someone is trying to poison me. For instance, every night after dinner I experience blurred vision and swelling. And all I've done is drink a bottle of red wine and eat twenty-three sausages.

Perhaps this is why Jocasta has instituted a weekday program of strictly-limited alcohol and low-fat food; a program which has done nothing except focus my mind firmly on the kitchen cupboard.

As I stand there, quietly whimpering, I consider the strange rules of food and drink. Isn't it time someone catalogued their eternal laws?

1. Food, if eaten straight from the cupboard, with the cupboard door still open, and no attempt to sit down, doesn't count in any calorie-control program.
2. Beer tastes worse with every additional glass, while red wine tastes better.

3. Broken biscuits, found in the bottom of the Tupperware, contain no calories.

4. Encouraging others to eat heartily is not only good manners. Over time, you'll start to look thin in comparison.

5. There is no point to the Brussels sprout.

6. There is never any room in the fridge, but nothing worth eating in there either.

7. If oysters weren't so expensive, people would realise they look like snot.

8. Every food cupboard has one obscure cooking ingredient in massive oversupply. You ran out of it once, and now buy a fresh packet on every supermarket visit. In our house, it's slivered almonds. We now have six small packs, enough to last, on current use, the next fifteen years.

9. UHT stands for Ultra Horrible Taste.

10. The favourite recipe of the serious cook always demands '¼ glass of good-quality white wine', thus forcing the opening of a bottle well before the arrival of the guests.

11. A watched bottle of white wine, slung in the freezer, never cools.

12. Eating healthy vegetables provides negative calories, allowing you to eat extra junk.

13. With every kilometre you drive further from Sydney's trendiest suburbs, the definition shifts of 'rare', 'medium rare' and 'well done'. Ask for 'rare' in Balmain, and they'll wipe its arse and plate it. Ask for 'rare' in Broken Hill and the cook will come out of the kitchen and give you a long hard stare.

14. When cooking for friends, put the most effort into the starter. They'll be too drunk to notice the dessert.
15. Left-overs of Chinese take-away should never be thrown out on the night. They should be put in the fridge for three weeks, and thrown out once they start growing.
16. The dessert stomach is a separate stomach. The main stomach may well be full after a huge main course, but the dessert stomach will still be empty, and demanding food. Indeed, some Sydney gourmands are equipped, cow-like, with at least four separate stomachs. The entrée stomach, the main meal stomach, the dessert stomach, and (hence the term) the petit-four stomach.
17. Hard-cover recipe books with titles like *Recipes from a Tuscan Garden*, equipped with gorgeous photos and exquisite prose, are never used. All your actual recipes come from a magazine-style compendium called *Bog in Quick*.
18. Milk tastes best when drunk straight from the carton at two in the morning.
19. Yuppie 'premium lager' beer such as Cascade and James Boag should *not* be consumed while watching Rugby League. Remember the rule of etiquette: 'It is offensive to drink from a bottle with a longer neck than the footballer you are cheering.'
20. No-one wants to eat the last stale handful of cornflakes in the box, yet no-one is allowed to throw them out either. Most families ban the

opening of a new box until the old is finished — forcing all family members to sullenly eat toast for four weeks until Mum relents.

21. Up the back of every kitchen cupboard is a sad stack of Indian spices from four years back when you bought an Indian cookbook. Throw them out now! Go on! Do it!

22. Recipe books always give a cooking time that is far too short. They also claim a given recipe will feed ten, when you would be lucky to get a meal for two wafer-thin monks. Either all recipe writers are extremely thin people with faulty ovens, or the rest of us are fat greedy pigs with faulty ovens. The oven manufactures must investigate.

23. Squares of chocolate, broken off the bar, are rounded down to include only the full squares.

24. In the search for that final bottle of beer, late at night, it is common to get up from the couch and search the fridge at least five times — in the hope that, in the two minutes since you last lifted up the bag of carrots, some sort of miracle may have taken place. This has never been known to happen.

25. And, finally but crucially: whiskey is always a mistake.

The Fall Guy

Friends can be cruel. At Jocasta's birthday party, they'd all combined to buy her a folding wooden chair, a lovely thing, which she could use when sitting outside in the sun, dreaming of what her life might have been. And so she sat on the chair and laughed at how great it was, and the friends smiled and drank her health, and then, yes, I too was invited to sit, and relaxed into the slatted frame, my drink held high.

Which is the point at which the whole thing collapsed. Not just broke. Shattered. From Elegant Chair to Pile of Splintered Firewood, it made its journey in half a second, leaving me sprawled on the floor, limbs akimbo, the drink flung from my hand, the friends caught between horror and laughter.

It was Jeff who broke the silence with a droll whisper: 'Meet Richard, the Man Mountain.'

A few of them laughed, which instantly warmed Jeff, a natural show-off, to his theme. The chair was made in Vietnam, and as I staggered to my feet he was busy painting a word picture of the moment of its construction — the villagers summoning the fattest man in the district to test the thing out, perhaps perching a child or two on

106

his lap, the timbers taking the enormous weight without complaint, the package being stamped for export.

'They'd have never dreamt of a bloke with an arse like yours,' Jeff said with a quiet, sad shrug. 'Not in their wildest dreams.'

It was most unfair. Later, after they'd all had their fun and left with their cheeks aching from laughter, I reconstructed the shattered mess as best I could. Obviously, this was not a case of an overweight passenger, but of inadequate gluing and poor design.

Yet still I have to face Jocasta, as she examines the almost inconceivable collapse — not so much that of the chair, as that of her husband's once-svelte body.

What's worse? Is it the way she weeps over the broken present, or the way she now flinches each time I lower myself into a chair, expecting the engineering to be unequal to its task? The standard of Vietnamese glue has a lot to answer for.

In an effort to save my battered dignity, I begin a campaign: all modern furniture is made of the thinnest pieces of wood and plastic, and all of it is portion-controlled and miserly. To prove my point, I take Jocasta on a tour of the flat-pack, build-yourself, furniture which we bought just months ago at Cheap and Nasty World — all of it already trashed, the melamine peeling, the drawers sagging, the chipboard swelling. Other people's surfaces may be distressed; ours are merely distressing.

And that's aside from the trauma I went through putting the stuff together, connecting Bolt A to Sprocket B via Nervous Breakdown C.

Suddenly, in the middle of Batboy's bedroom, staring at his stricken bedside table, I come over all philosophical

— wondering why nothing's built to last, how we're increasingly living in a world built of lattice and Gyprock, of melamine and plastic drawer-runners, and how the throwaway society has finally engulfed our furniture and even our architecture.

My heart was full, my buttocks a-quiver, and I said it all. Jocasta endured the full oration, an eyebrow cocked in amusement. 'Maybe you should hop down off your soapbox, now,' she said finally, 'before it splinters under your weight.'

This is what I get these days, my friends lying in wait to make some cheap joke; some one-liner about the killer bum; the man of the mighty beam, striding through life, making furniture-owners everywhere tremble.

'Sit down, Richard,' they'll say, 'we need some firewood.'

Or, 'Richard's coming over, better reinforce the porch.'

Or, 'Just perch on the bed, mate — I'm trying to convert it into a futon.'

And so I dream of that glorious prelapsarian time, the time before my bottom became literally the butt of jokes. Back then, before the Fall.

Backyard Cricket

There's a moment in the development of every great sport when the rules are written down and formalised, and surely that time has arrived for the game of backyard cricket.

The Rules of Backyard Cricket

1. There shall be no golden ducks. Here, if nowhere else in life, you always get a second go.
2. The wicket shall be constructed of any material, yet tradition prefers a garbage tin. It is noted: the arrival of the wheelie bin in the suburbs is already creating a new generation of bowlers — ones who'll forever believe the stumps are shoulder height, and a good metre wide.
3. The pitch shall vary between 33 yards and 11, depending on the intoxication of those marking it out.
4. A batsman shall be deemed 'Not Out' if the ball hits the top of the garbage bin.
5. Younger players, defined as under eight years, will be permitted to weep upon getting out. They

should then refuse to give back the bat, running haphazardly away, as their father chases angrily after them, shouting entreaties. This is known as the on-field entertainment.

6. The game shall consist of 'hit-and-run' — once the bat touches the ball, you've got to run. We haven't got all day for this game: there's still stuff to eat in the Esky.

7. The middle-aged uncle who was once the glory of the school cricket team is permitted one full-speed, lairy bowl during the afternoon — smashing the wickets of his eleven-year-old nephew — just to show he's still got it.

8. The middle-aged uncle should not be criticised for this behaviour. Tomorrow's herniated disc will be deemed punishment enough.

9. A ball bouncing off a roof must be caught one-handed. Fielders may wish to equip themselves with a plastic cup of riesling, held in the left hand, as protection from inadvertently breaking this rule.

10. Nanna, while fierce with a bat, shall be permitted to utilise a runner, chosen from the younger members of the group. Thus is speed combined with wisdom.

11. It shall be permitted for the bowler to soak the tennis ball in a nearby puddle in order to add both speed and drama, particularly when employing a Bodyline strategy.

12. Should a seven-year-old score more than twenty runs it is permitted to distract the child,

claiming the sound of a Mr Whippy van can be heard in the middle distance.

13. If the ball is driven into a wire fence, becoming stuck, fielders may remove it one-handed for the 'Out'. Who ever said life was fair?

14. Over the fence is 'Six — and Out'. If the batter cannot locate the ball, he may be derided as a lair and a show-off by all present.

15. When playing with limited numbers, the system of 'Automatic Slips' may be instituted, in which any ball hit towards the slips will be deemed caught.

16. Some players believe 'Automatic Slips' removes human error from the game. Such players may prefer to play 'English Team Rules' in which every ball hit towards the slips is deemed dropped.

17. Balls which become stuck in trees are deemed caught. By Joel Garner if the tree is tall.

18. In games with limited fieldsmen, and a single, difficult-to-defeat batter, one may institute the system of 'electric wickets', meaning they can be run-out by hitting either wicket, and not just the one towards which they are running.

19. Any on-field mistake shall be greeted with the dismissive chorus from all players: 'Can't bowl, can't field.' Players who are incompetent, and miss every ball, should insist they are in the pay of Salim Malik and are intentionally 'throwing the game'.

20. It's acknowledged that backyard cricket is an excellent guide to a person's basic character.

Will the sixteen-year-old give the ball a sweet nudge towards the great-grandparent fielding at silly point? Or go the full lobotomy shot in the hope of an early inheritance? Only backyard cricket will tell.

21. Suspect bowling actions will be frowned upon, in particular those made without a can of beer in one hand. As Shoaib Akhtar might put it: 'There's plenty of scope for chucking later in the night.'

22. Runs will be subtracted for hitting the ball into the wood pile (due to fear of snakes); or into Uncle Terry's new car (due to fear of Uncle Terry).

23. The dog will be considered an act of God — his actions bringing a much-needed measure of pure luck to a game too long mired in skill.

24. The intelligent son-in-law will unaccountably 'miss' the bails several times during Pa's innings. He shall remember that Christmas is close, and that Pa's traditional gift of red wine may be selected from the Over $15 section, or from the Under $5.

25. After the sixteen-year-old has achieved twenty-five runs, he may be openly mocked and derided, and forced to hit a dolly towards Nanna, which she will catch with a long, dramatic, but ultimately bone-cracking dive towards silly leg.

Backyard cricket again reveals the family secret: those idiotically competitive genes came from someplace.

Stark Staring

It was Batboy who had the insight. The grand moment of vision. We'd gone to the Art Gallery, attracted by the new gallery of traditional painting. But first, we thought, we should head downstairs and introduce Batboy to some contemporary art. In particular those rocks they've got on the ground floor, all hanging in a circle from the ceiling.

Whenever you look at contemporary art, there's always someone in the background mumbling that 'a child could do better', so this was the perfect opportunity to see whether an actual young person agreed.

Batboy, as it happens, adjudged himself quite unable to do any better and was very admiring of the circle of hanging rocks — especially its capacity to be used as a weapon. But the interesting moment happened when we clambered towards the traditional paintings, and Batboy made his announcement: compared with that sensible modern stuff downstairs, this lot was, well, kind of weird.

Jocasta and I examined the paintings, and you could see his point. The joint is full of the odder outpourings of the pre-modern mind: unicorns, nymphs, crucifixes, men with animal bodies, severed heads on trays, and a veritable plague of stags and lutes. Traditional painters are very big on lutes.

There's all this moaning about the weirdness of modern art, but when you finally open your eyes, you find a striking and beautiful circle of stones. Not weird at all.

Meanwhile, upstairs, is your typical traditional painting, and it will feature a bloke with goat legs, suckling a devil with his engorged breast (oh, didn't I mention the breasts?) while somebody in the background has his head hacked off with a sword. Batboy is right. It's sicko stuff. Enter it in the Biennale and they'd be denouncing you as a typical sybaritic modernist.

And then I notice this other thing about the galleries of traditional art. All the women are in the nude. You'll have these groups of people, doing something quite ordinary, like cooking a meal or hacking the festering head off a succubus, and all the men will be in full ceremonial dress while the women, whoops, they've somehow forgotten to put on their shirts.

Oddest of all, they don't even bother explaining why the women are naked. They just are. On principle.

At least today's film-makers contrive a storyline to get their female stars naked ('Scene Five: Sharon decides her turtle-neck sweater is so hot she'd best remove it.') But not these people. They can be painting a woman welding the back axle of her oxcart, and they'll think: 'Just as easy to make her starkers.'

It's like the famous painting by Manet, *Le Dejeuner sur l'Herbe*. Here's a group of friends; they've decided to have a picnic; they've spread out the rug; the blokes are dressed to kill, and everybody's getting stuck right into the King Island brie and the Rosemount chardonnay.

And what does the woman in the picture decide to do? Naturally, she elects to strip off and plonk herself starkers right there among the plastic plates, happy as Larry.

We blokes have seen the painting at school. We have studied the poster on kitchen walls. And we've gone on about 4 000 picnics ever since, always with that vague sense of hope.

Our conclusion? Manet must have been running with a crowd of sheilas somewhat different to the ones who attend our picnics.

Or take another example — the famous Sid Long painting of the pink flamingos. It's got two women and they are watching a glorious flock of pink flamingos, and so what do they do to increase their viewing pleasure? Off come the duds. Stark naked is the only way to get a good viewing of a flamingo, and why don't all the zoo's female patrons realise it?

Surely, the good news is the popularity of artists such as Robert Mapplethorpe, in whose work it is almost always the men who are walking around naked. Men oiling up their bodies and flexing with pride. Men removing their clothes at the slightest provocation. Men staring at themselves in the mirror and going: 'Um, not bad.'

It's taken centuries to get here. But at least some art seems to be recording the day-to-day realities of your typical Australian suburban home.

The Scapie

Occasionally, while cooking, I'm forced to ask the odd question. For instance: 'Who the bloody hell has hidden the garlic crusher, since it's supposed to be right here in the second drawer?' In response, Jocasta usually points out there are only two people who use the garlic crusher. Her. And me. Which means my question is not a question at all. But rather a thinly veiled accusation.

Jocasta reckons men are always asking these sort of 'questions' — questions like 'Who's lost my keys?', 'Who's moved my bag?' and 'Who's broken the washing machine?' Questions to which the men clearly feel they already have the answer. We might believe we are launching a speculative inquiry, but all Jocasta sees is a nation of Emile Zolas, shouting *'J'accuse'* over the kitchen bench.

Take last week, when we were finishing off the new bathroom. I'd climbed down the ladder, tripped over my open tool box and was busy being catapulted head-first towards the still-talking toilet. Naturally, as I came to rest on the ground, I put the question. 'Who,' I said, 'put my bloody tool box right at the foot of the bloody ladder?'

It was just a general non-specific, open-ended question. But since Jocasta and I were the only ones in the room, it may have had just a hint of '*J'accuse*'.

Jocasta, slowly, carefully, began to answer. And I was shocked. For the first time in our years together, she was giving the answer for which my question clearly yearned.

'I did it,' said Jocasta. 'It was my fault. You weren't to know I'd moved it. And into such an idiotic place. And now, of course, I feel so stupid. And the thought that you, darling, may have been hurt ...'

It was great hearing those words — those tender, blame-accepting words — but it didn't take long for me to hear a cautionary voice in the back of my head. A voice that said: 'Mate, beware, for I think she may very well be taking the piss.'

And thus, verily, did it come to pass.

Jocasta, surrounded by sheets of tongue-in-groove panelling, had now taken to waving a sharp chisel in my direction. 'Suddenly it's become clear,' she said, 'the importance of my role. I'm the scapegoat. The person who takes the blame off the others. I mean, look at the team of tradesmen on your typical building site — you've got the brickie, the chippie and the sparkie. And then the scapie. The scapegoat.

'And, let's face it, the scapie may well be the most important role of all. The chippie may stop the ceiling collapsing. But the scapie stops the *chippie* collapsing — we buttress his ego, we are the massive bearers who take the strain of his mistakes.'

I decided to retaliate: 'Look, I merely asked ...'

'No', said Jocasta, 'I'm not upset, I merely want recognition for the role — for all we scapies, both male

117

and female, at home and in business. I want recognition for the service we provide. Like the salesman in the small company, the bloke who gets blamed by the boss and everyone else for the turndown in the business; every time things get tense, every time they consider sacking everyone and reorganising the firm, the cry will go up, "But it's all Gordon's fault".'

Jocasta explained: 'Gordon's the scapie, and if you think about it, he's the one bloke holding that place together. And then there's your domestic scapies, heroically taking the blame. The bloke burns the casserole? Ah, says the scapie, I should have alerted you to the proper cooking temperature.

'Or the bloke who backs the Falcon up the driveway, drunk, and knocks in the fence? My fault for not moving the fence a little to the left.'

I decided to sit down on my tool box and take a lower profile.

'Mate,' continued Jocasta, letting loose her tool belt, 'I'd just like to see some recognition. Like today. Without a good scapie like me, you'd lose your confidence. You wouldn't be able to continue in the delusion that you're a good builder, tragically saddled with an incompetent helper.'

Jocasta smiled one of her fabulous smiles, and I decided it was best to get on with things — measuring a fresh bit of panelling, and sawing it off according to my template.

I went to hammer it in, and Jocasta and I both instantly spotted the problem. 'No way,' she said rapidly, 'could you have been so stupid as to saw that angle the wrong way round, totally wasting the piece of wood. I mean, only a total idiot would do that. Nah, it must have been my fault. The way I completely distracted you with all that talk.'

I looked up at my life-partner, and met her blue eyes, which were alive with a twinkle I have long learnt to fear. 'You see,' she said, in a secretive whisper, 'I really am the world's best scapie.'

Rules of Life

There are many scientific rules that affect ordinary life, so isn't it time we collected the most significant dozen?

Rule 1: The uglier the couch, the more comfort it provides

One of the great, overriding laws of the universe, right up there with $E = mc^2$. Sink into a truly ugly couch, and instantly you feel the difference: the comforting orange velour covering; the low-slung sprawl of its cushions; the groaning springs which bow to your superior weight. The truly fashionable, meanwhile, find themselves perched aboard something sleek and Italian, the upholstery so taut it could repel bullets.

Even in city restaurants, this law works its magic. Hence the sub-law: the more expensive the restaurant, the less comfortable the chairs. Oh, for a top-notch eatery fitted out with vinyl-upholstered booths.

Rule 2: The more hideous the sock, the more likely it is to last forever

I spend half my life buying pairs of stylish cotton business socks. Within weeks, only one of them is left, the other is missing in action or full of holes. But here is a curious fact: ugly, nylon socks never leave you. Make a rash purchasing error in 1977 — something nylon, something tartan, something perhaps with writing on it — and there it will be twenty years on, winking at you from your sock drawer, demanding to be worn to work every Friday, when all other contenders are gone.

Rule 3: A spoon, placed at random on a kitchen sink, will automatically position itself under the tap

Who knows why, but turn on the tap at full blast and every spoon within 50 metres will have positioned itself beneath the torrent. The effect: a wide-arching spray of scalding water all over the washer-up.

Rule 4: With processed food, hope springs eternal

The frozen lasagne. The microwavable pizza. The dried pasta product: 'Just add water and you've got Spaghetti Carbonara that a restaurant would serve.' So many products, so many promises — and so many bitter disappointments.

Yet how quickly we forget. My hand pauses at the supermarket freezer, hovering over the frozen Meat Pie and Vegetables Family Dinner. *How bad can it be?* Two hours later we eat, and discover the answer: very bad indeed. But, somehow, the next week Jocasta and I are back, behind the trolley, lingering at the freezers. We're like Adam and Eve — before that first bite of Frozen Apple Pie Surprise, innocent in the face of experience: 'I mean, how bad ...'

Rule 5: Men are genetically incapable of reading a recipe to the end before they start cooking

This explains why, when waiting at the dining table for a gentleman host to serve his meal, guests will often hear a scream of rage at about 8.00 p.m. It marks the moment he has turned over the cookbook's page and seen for the first time: 'Step 4, simmer gently for six hours.'

Rule 6: The comfort and contentment of any baby is in inverse proportion to that of the adult holding it

Only when you are standing on one leg, leaning to the left and rocking backwards will a baby consider stopping crying.

Rule 7: Toilets are all designed so the lid will not stay upright of its own accord, but instead hovers precariously before slamming shut at the worst possible moment

This is the primary cause of nervous illness among the male population. And of wet toilet seats.

Rule 8: The phone only ever rings when you are sitting down to dinner

This is completely unlike the doorbell, which only ever rings when you are in the shower. People who crave human contact should instantly retire to the shower with their dinner.

Rule 9: The more sport your children play, the more unhealthy you'll become

All children's sport in Australia has the same fundraising method: the sausage sizzle. They play; you eat. Thus the strange outcome: the fitter they get, the fatter you'll get.

Rule 10: Photocopy machines never work

This shows how technology has gone downhill since the days of the reliable Roneo machine. (Thus giving rise to the common office cry: 'Wherefore art thou, Roneo?')

Rule 11: Radio news bulletins of great personal interest are only ever broadcast when your car is about to enter a tunnel

The broadcast is always cut off one and a half seconds after entering the tunnel and will resume on the last word as you leave it.

Rule 12: The more times you hear the phrase 'your call is important to us', the less important it actually is

I *could* go on. For instance: 'The more inaccessible the light bulb, the more often it will need to be changed.' Or, 'The nicer the shirt, the more likely the pen will leak in the top pocket.' Or, 'The chance of a baby throwing up on its parent's shoulder rises with the cost of the garment being worn.'

But, as scientists would know, this can only ever be a partial list. We'll call you for more suggestions next time you're sitting down to dinner.

5

Jocasta, cleaning out the laundry, discovers we don't actually have three ironing baskets. We have *four*. And this one has been sitting around for months. It's the Ironing Basket of Death. It's the Too-Hard Basket.

Interior Monologue

I'm kneeling on the bathroom floor, a virtual human sacrifice, armed only with a rolled-up copy of *Home Style Today* magazine. In front of me, an outstretched arm away, is our washing machine — 60 kilos of hulking rust, water and malevolence — about to enter a spin cycle of quite frightening abandon.

As it picks up speed, it starts to shake and shudder and thud, almost jitterbugging toward the door. It's a big fat square of white and chrome, busy shaking itself to death — sort of like Elvis in 1977.

Right now I'm trying to stuff the copy of *Home Style Today* under Elvis's front left leg. My aim is to achieve some sort of stability, despite a bathroom floor which is full of sudden depressions. Much like its owners.

The washing machine, it seems clear, has a different aim: to crush me into a bloodied pulp and leave me dead against the bathroom wall. I heave upwards and start pushing the *Home Style Today* under Elvis's leg; the magazine ripping a little so that I can see a few flashes of its contents. Azure pools. Sunday brunches. Found objects.

'Back, damn you,' I mutter as I shove, my cheek pressed up against Elvis's shuddering side, my frontal lobes getting a most attention-grabbing work-over. '*A Whole Lotta Shakin' Going On*'.

The way I've folded the magazine, a typical *Home Style Today* article faces upwards as I push it into place: 'It's easy', it says, 'to achieve a sophisticated but relaxed lifestyle'.

I don't quite know why Jocasta and I buy these magazines. In theory it's to get home-making tips. But the main 'tip', it always turns out, is to have about five million dollars and a team of decorators and tradesmen. Certainly that's what everyone featured in the magazine has done.

Take this particular article, on top of which Elvis's leg is currently shuddering. Brett and Veronica, of Darling Point, have recently decided to build a waterfront home of first-class design, with stables, pool and en suite granny mansion. Interestingly, it appears that Brett is heir to the SaltyBitz snack-food empire, while Veronica's a freelance design consultant who's done groundbreaking work in the area of bathroom vanities, and is closely related to the Queen of Sheba.

Must I read on? I must. My head is face down, pressed toward the article, as I struggle with the shuddering Pelvis, my knees sinking into that dip in the bathroom floor where the kids' bathwater always collects.

The photographs show a house slightly larger than the Sydney Football Stadium, equipped with virtually no furniture, save for a couple of chairs manufactured by the Danish Torture Commission. As chairs go they are very minimalist. *Very* minimalist. In fact, they're just two radiata posts, placed casually onto the floor, above which guests are meant to hover. A snip at $2 000 each. As Veronica simpers:

'To strip furniture back like that, to its very essence, to its very piece-of-woodiness, well, naturally it costs a little.'

Veronica describes her house as 'cosy — a real traditional home', later providing her own special definition of 'cosy': 'It's a place where one can easily invite 260 close friends to an impromptu performance of *Aida*, and still have room for a horse race down the hall.'

As you might expect, Brett and Veronica's children are all above average. I give another shove against Elvis's flank, and find myself remembering a book I once saw. Something like: *How to Increase Your IQ by Eating Gifted Children*. Thank goodness Veronica, with her usual flair, has chosen to house the children in their own wing, nestled by the harbour.

Suddenly, I feel I have a lot in common with Veronica, as our shuddering washing machine starts spewing water from its innards, cascading over my legs.

'There you are, Veronica,' I think, with just that little bit of pride, staring down at my soaked jeans, 'you're not the only one close to the water.'

The washing machine starts spasming, banging against the peeling paint on the bathroom wall, before the spin cycle finally stops. I relax, allowing my head to loll against Elvis's still warm flank. Idly, I wonder where Veronica's machine comes from. Probably Sweden.

People talk about the shattering effect of the cover-girl supermodels on the body-image of normal women; but what about the effect of a single issue of *Home Style Today* on our domestic morale? Perhaps I need a new magazine, more tailored to my lifestyle. Something like *Bad Housekeeping*. Or *Slacker Homes and Gardens*. Or *Home Bludger*.

I pat Elvis's flank and start to remove the clothes, which I must say he has washed superbly.

Veronica's house — and washing machine — may be elegant, but sometimes, particularly at wash time, it's not so bad to have some real agitation.

WebbyNettyStuff

For a few years now, the world has seen an exponential growth in web-sites and e-businesses — all united by the desire to print EverySecond WordTogether for no DiscernibleReason.

But surely we need even more such businesses — all helping yet more people replace real experiences with web-potato ones.

SmellTheRoses.com At SmellTheRoses we interrupt your work every half-hour, replacing your current Net page with a high-resolution picture of a rose, thus forcing you to take a break and it least *see* the roses. Voted Most Annoying Web Service four years running.

VirusRenamer@CyberSisterhood.com Here at CyberSisterhood we can't understand why computer viruses all have female names, when it's male computer nerds who've caused the problem. Talk about typical! Our VirusRenamer searches the Net and gives trouble its correct name — Barry, Steve or Brian.

EmptyCupboard.com At EmptyCupboard we realise Internet shopping is a lot of overhyped bull: it takes hours, a gormless sixteen-year-old mispacks your order, and — due to a mistaken keystroke — you've inevitably ordered nothing but a 75 kilo crate of dried basil. At EmptyCupboard we help the failed Internet shopper with recipes based entirely on all that's left in your cupboard — a bag of rice and an old tin of Irish Stew. Enjoy!

PeskyKids.com Perhaps your kids don't bother you any more because their heads are in the Net. Why not download some PeskyKids! We interrupt your own work on the Net with flashed requests for biscuits, drinks, and company. Both of you might be working on separate computers, in separate rooms, but with PeskyKids you can still imagine what a real family would be like.

And coming soon for kids: AuthoritarianDad.com This cyber-father actually supervises your Web use instead of just downloading porn in his own room. Hours of RealFeel Conflict! Adds RebelliousFeel to Web use.

TimeFiller@TelstraBigPond.com Here at Telstra's BigPond we're sick of Regional and Rural customers and their whingeing and whining about how long it takes to download a single Net page over our antiquated phone lines. That's why we're going to make some changes. Post us a letter outlining your problem, and we'll send you a paperback copy of Tolstoy's *War and Peace* — absolutely ready-to-read as you wait. No more wasted download TelstraHours!

ChatWithStyle.com We've spent hours monitoring Yahoo's teenage chat rooms, and despaired at the poor level of conversation. Sure, young people of all nations are meeting, but what are they saying to each other? Stuff like: 'Hellllo?' and 'Anyone there????' and 'Who else likes Britney Spears???' Download our ConversationFilter, and everything changes. Type in the question 'Anyone else like Manchester FC?', and our filter automatically turns it into a knowledgeable inquiry about their last game with Leeds. Mention Dannii Minogue, and our ConversationFilter simply turns it into an inquiry about the more sophisticated Macy Gray. Don't just lie about your age, gender and occupation; lie about your sense of style as well.

SpeechAtDad'sFuneral.com In the busy go-ahead world of e-commerce, who's got time for parents? Especially when they show how very OldWorld they are by actually dying. Log onto our site, add a few details such as your dad's name and hobby, and our DeepFeelings software will produce a moving elegy. Download us before you Download Dad.

WebbyNettyStuff@ComputerBS.com How can you get a groovy name for your web-site? A name like goFish, Excite or Yahoo. Just visit us here at WebbyNettyStuff. Remember how the Web works — it's full of giant, grey-suited multinationals pretending to be groovy adolescents. Our principle: the bigger your company, the more childish the name. That way no-one will catch on to the truth — that the groovy new economy is exactly the same as the old: lots of money being made by a few multinationals. Don't tell anyone, now.

EmailCrusader.com Many companies are now generating so much internal e-mail, that no actual work takes place. At EmailCrusader we've discovered the rule: the more boring the department, the more e-mail it generates. In most companies, 95 per cent of all e-mails are generated by the Training Department, the Fire Drill Department, and the computer section itself. EmailCrusader disconnects them every time they try to communicate with the outside world. Voted Web-Site Most Likely To Stop Everyone Going Insane.

HateSmugComputerBastard.com We're a flame site for those sick of computer nerds. We maintain that content is more important than the delivery system; that the invention of the Web is less important than the discovery of the yo-yo; and that people with an excessive belief in the transforming power of the Net are all nerds. Voted Least Visited Site twenty years running. Which makes us *very* proud.

Free for All

The Space Cadet and I are lolling by the roadside, just shy of the gutter. We're seated in two large, stuffed armchairs, feeling like lords. The Space Cadet wriggles deeper into his recliner, noting how the back swivels for extra comfort.

It is then he utters the ominous words: 'Who'd chuck out this? You'd have to be mad.'

It means he's afflicted by the gene. The scrounger gene. The scavenger gene. Just like his father, he'll never be able to pass a garage sale, a council clean-up, or even a straight-out stinking tip, without stopping and having a poke around.

Right now, it's the mid-year Council Clean-Up, and it's a dangerous time to drive. The car in front will suddenly swerve toward the gutter, the driver entranced by the sight of an exhausted water heater, lying on its side, bleeding its yellow stuffing.

A clever bloke, they'll be thinking, could make something out of that.

Why do we do it? Not for any good reason. Oh, but the surge of good feeling as you first take away your find. The feeling that you've been able to spot rich possibilities where others couldn't.

- *You could turn that water heater into a cubby for the kids.*
- *You could put that three-legged table upside down and use it for quoits.*
- *You could take the engine out of that lawnmower and make a most attractive planter box.*

After some argument, I convince The Space Cadet to leave the torn, rank armchairs behind, and we move down the road. I notice he is skipping with joy. We pause and poke around the next pile. The Space Cadet looks up and says: 'I love doing this, Dad.'

He's got it bad.

Someone's chucked out an old, broken, black and white portable TV. It's exactly the same as our own black and white TV — the one I'd been contemplating throwing out myself. I have to fight the urge to take it home. Thus the rule: something you'd instantly chuck if found under your own bed, becomes a sparkling jewel when chucked out by another.

A roll of wire, an old pram, a broken cupboard with good handles, a busted ping-pong table: all are taken in, before good sense revolts. Next year, on Clean-Up Day, they'll go out once again, only to be picked up by another. Just like the busted-up exercise bike I swear's been circling the suburb for years, providing more exercise through lifting and carrying than it ever has through pedalling.

Yet who can resist the urge? A brass porthole? Walk past it, and the very next week an obscure uncle will die in South Africa, leaving you his steamboat — in perfect condition save for the missing porthole. A roll of lino? *The very next day* the note comes home from school:

'As the children are practising stencilling, could each child bring a square of lino?'

A bit further down the street and The Space Cadet is suggesting we take home a large pile of still-green tree-prunings because 'they'd make good wood for the barbecue'. He is also keen on a milk-shake maker with broken glass and English electrical points.

He's starting to get a bit thin-lipped about the way I keep saying 'no' to all his great finds. 'You know, you're allowed to take it, Dad. You're allowed. It's the law.'

Next house along, he pushes aside a few polystyrene boxes, and spots a cricket bat — scuffed on the bottom, with some silver electrical tape clumped around the handle. By now, I'm in the habit of dissuading him. 'No, leave it alone, it's just rubbish.' But he reaches in, pulls it into the light and takes an experimental swing.

I have to admit, it's a beauty. An old well-made bat; the sticky and torn electrical tape easily removed. The Space Cadet puts on a mock-pompous voice: 'I think you better apologise to me for that. It's not rubbish at all.'

We take the bat home, full of the good times of the Council Clean-Up, talking of how we'll clean and sand and fix the bat until it's the best ever.

Yet, turning the corner, I realise that even this is not a time without shadows. Just before we left on our rounds — just an hour ago — I'd placed on the footpath my own pile of chuck-outs. Among them: the rusted metal bit from the wheel of a wheelbarrow long-gone.

It is gone. I stand there stunned. I have come face to face with the most powerful rule of Clean-Up Day: there is no realisation more gnawingly horrible than that someone saw possibility where you could see none.

Sold Short

The advertising industry has always been skilled at taking large quantities of its clients' money in return for slogans so lamebrained they could have been composed by a housebrick. But it's only in the last few years that the industry has fallen, slathering, onto the ultimate ruse, which is to convince its clients that the really *hip* commercials are the ones that say, 'Our product is so good, it doesn't need a slogan.'

This, they have realised, beats the hell out of staying up nights to find something to rhyme with McIntosh Nasi Goreng.

The clients seem to be falling for it, since half the nation's products now seem to have a no-slogan slogan. A Reebok campaign, for example, shows a series of not very good slogans, ending with the creative megawork: 'Reebok — no slogans.' Or, at least, 'Reebok — no slogans we could think of before we went to lunch and got stuck into the Tasmanian semillon.' What used to be the text of the apologetic telegram you'd send to the client — NO SLOGANS STOP WILL TRY AGAIN TOMORROW STOP — is now cheerfully presented as the campaign centrepiece.

Or take the Reschs Real ad, which offered the sheer genius of: 'With a beer this good, who needs clever advertising.' Which does rather suggest the rejoinder: 'With a slogan that bad, who needs an expensive ad agency.'

Advertising is only a lowly part of our modern culture. It's the small intestine of the body politic; the organ that finally digests developments in the high arts, and then turns them into ... well, waste. But the production of waste as toxic as the no-slogan slogan suggests serious problems in the higher organs.

Problems like the cult of irony — that post-modern love of knowingness, of self-consciousness, of the mocking half-parody, of embarrassment at admitting conviction or sincerity.

You shall know it from its offspring. Among them: the self-aware tonight show, full of knowing winks and smug self-parody; the self-aware country band, half-parodying the music it's playing; the self-aware building, loudly screeching its post-modern borrowings.

And, now, the self-aware advertisement — hiply admitting, for those too stupid to work it out themselves, that, yes, they are watching an advert.

Every age has its soft spot, its area of naivety, and this is ours: this tendency to mistake self-consciousness for honesty. When, instead, we should recognise it as an effort to beguile us further; and to dress up the crummy and the borrowed as things fresh and new.

I never warmed to the cult of irony, even when, a decade back, it was limited to the inner-city few — people who simply didn't have time, in their busy schedules of parties and put-downs, to develop their own ideas or beliefs. And so merely slipped into the pose of a weary and knowing detachment.

But it's even more unattractive now it's become just another mass-market stance — used to flog everything from tonight shows to shoes.

And could any irony be greater than this: that what began as a passionate and necessary debate among French structuralists about cultural relativism and our roles as the bearers of cultural ideas has ended up as a series of dopey country bands, shoe ads and bad tonight shows?

Is there any hope for Western civilisation after irony? We must take hope: surely once an idea is turning up in shoe ads, its time must be up. When irony and self-consciousness turn up in a commercial, it may mean they've finally arrived at the very end of the small intestine — and are about to be joyfully expelled into the dunny can of history.

With them gone, we can all fill up again — maybe even on sincerity, on commitment, on the search for values. And hope for a time in which architects, slogan writers, novelists, fashion designers, and tonight show hosts are expected to come up with their own ideas — and believe in them, too.

Wow, *post*-post-modernism. Now that *is* hip.

Dirt File

It is now essential for young men, moving out of home for the first time, to be able to fend for themselves. As a one-time Young Male Slob, I am in a position to offer this cut-out-and-keep manual: 'The Idiot's Guide to Domestic Life'. Pin it up for the slobby bachelor boy (or slobby bachelor girl) near you.

Clothes Washing

Suggest to a Typical Young Man that he should wear the same underpants two days running, and he'll be horrified. Instead, he'll take off his underpants, leave them on the bedroom floor for a week and a half, and then he'll wear them again.

This is their point: Typical Young Men do not believe clothes need to be washed. They believe they need to be *rested*. They think their undies have just got all hot and sweaty, and all they need to do is calm down, take it easy, maybe just slob around lying on the floor for a week or two, and — fantastic — they'll be ready for another outing.

And the same goes for work pants, favourite T-shirts and — in older men — dinner suits, which, with proper rest, can go for decades (even, in later years, attending many functions unaccompanied).

Typical Young Men, you understand, have not yet heard about washing. When they lived at home, they just placed their clothes on the floor of the bedroom and then found them, some days later, washed and ironed and hanging up. But, sometime or other, we are going to have to break the bad news: The Clothes Did Not Achieve This Unaided. Somebody helped them do it. And they did it by using The Big White Shaky Machine inside the Room With Tiles.

Washing Up

When moving into his own place, the Typical Young Man may be surprised to find that dirty plates and cups begin to accumulate on the metal thing in the kitchen ('the sink').

These need to be washed. For this you need to dress like a cautious surgeon, wearing thick rubber gloves, a protective apron and — sure, if you feel like it — a condom certainly wouldn't do any harm.

The trick is to immerse the dirty plates in hot water and sort of rub them with the wet thing ('the sponge'). If that doesn't work, you can try rubbing them with the scratchy thing ('the scratchy thing'). Shocking fact, but true: this has to be repeated daily.

The good news is that if you still can't get

something clean you should 'leave it to soak'. This is Young Guy language for: 'Janice can do it later'.

Ironing

Typical Young Men always try to take short cuts with ironing. They'll do the front of a shirt, then skip the back. They figure they'll be wearing a jacket anyway so who will know? In winter months, they've even been known — OK, I've even been known — to just iron the collar and a sort of V-shaped area on the front, and count on the sweater to cover the rest.

But ironing a shirt properly is not that hard. Just select the correct temperature, and remember the Idiot's First Law of Ironing: if the shirt you're ironing has very, very long sleeves, it may well be a pair of pants.

Cleaning the Floor

Before vacuuming your new place, you'll have to figure out what sort of floor covering you are dealing with, which can be tough in a house full of Typical Young Men.

Look down at your floor right now, and describe the major floor covering. That's right — empty pizza boxes and grease-covered motorcycle parts. But now, try looking under the pizza boxes and the bike parts. Yes! You have a floor! And a vermin problem! What a shame that man, like nature, abhors a vacuum.

Cooking

It's not as hard as it looks. At each meal, just eat something from each major food type:

1. Food from cupboards;
2. Food from fridges;
3. Food you ring up for;
4. Beer.

The rules of cooking are very easy. Food from cupboards is boiled or heated and food from fridges is grilled or fried. Food from cupboards is technically known as carbohydrate, and includes pasta, rice and potatoes. Food from fridges, on the other hand, is always protein — unless it's green coloured, in which case it's usually just some very off meat. Or, in very rare cases, a vegetable.

Either way, the Typical Young Man will refuse to eat it. The need to 'get plenty of greens' can be addressed by opening another can of VB.

Cleaning the Bathroom

Many Typical Young Men are shocked to find that cleaning a bathroom doesn't just mean flushing the loo. And so they sit, staring at the disgraceful mess, hopefully wondering if 'Putrid Black' is just another designer colour in the Fowler Ware range.

They should think again — and leave the room locked and barred for at least a week. Like their undies, it may need a thorough resting.

The Baby Club

The baby club, and sometimes the two-baby club, is gaining plenty of new celebrity members. Demi Moore, Madonna and Annette Bening, among others. A few years back even Michael Jackson was achieving fatherhood — a conception presumably designed to defy *pre*-conceptions.

Babies, it now seems, are the latest fashion accessory for Hollywood stars — the perfect reaction either to that fading career, or to those troublesome allegations.

But, for stars, the experience of bringing up baby is surely a little different to the norm — right from the moment they first book into the LA birth centre, that cervix station to the stars.

Celebrity parents are suddenly everywhere, but could you qualify? Try our quick quiz.

When my baby cries out, I usually awaken:

- (a) immediately;
- (b) almost immediately;
- (c) after a few moments;
- (d) the nanny and the rest of her night staff.

I define a child restraint as:

(a) a car seat;
(b) a baby capsule;
(c) a condom;
(d) the electric fence between the nanny's cottage and the main residence.

The first photos of my baby were taken:

(a) on his rug;
(b) in the bath;
(c) at the hospital;
(d) from my bag by the nanny, and then sold to *New Idea*.

When I was pregnant, I always appeared:

(a) very tired;
(b) quite bloated;
(c) a little flushed;
(d) stark naked on the cover of *Vanity Fair*.

My spare time is constantly spent expressing:

(a) milk;
(b) myself.

I see my child as a way of gaining more:

(a) meaning in my life;
(b) joy in small things;

(c) balance between work and play;
(d) cheap publicity.

How often does your child wear you out?

(a) never, I'm the complete mother;
(b) sometimes, especially when he's teething;
(c) always — I'm a wreck;
(d) I'm sorry, there must be some mistake: nanny dresses him in blue, I wear pink, the paparazzi gather ... and I wear *him* out.

I'm working hard to get my child to establish his own routine:

(a) at bedtime;
(b) at mealtime;
(c) at bathtime;
(d) at Caesar's Palace.

By the time he's two years old, I'd love to see my child moving:

(a) his legs and arms;
(b) his facial muscles;
(c) his neck;
(d) into his own condo.

I define 'gross motor skills' as the moment my child:

(a) grasped a pencil;
(b) lifted a spoon;

(c) connected some Lego;

(d) threw up in the back of the limo.

If my child does anything wrong, I force him to spend time:

(a) standing in the corner;

(b) sitting in his room;

(c) thinking at his desk;

(d) dining back in economy.

I never leave home without my:

(a) nappy bag;

(b) travel cot;

(c) baby wipes;

(d) entourage.

This is a child conceived:

(a) in a moment of passion;

(b) on the back seat of a Holden;

(c) because of a life commitment;

(d) by my press agent.

The last time my child ate all his dinner, I was in a state:

(a) of bliss;

(b) of relief;

(c) of smug parental satisfaction;

(d) somewhere in the Midwest. Probably Idaho. On the new Coen brothers film.

In attempting toilet training, I always:

(a) let him choose his own time;
(b) put him on the toilet and wait;
(c) use small bribes;
(d) cheer when anything happens — it's always been the reaction to my own, very similar, productions.

Scoring: Score four points for every (d) answer. In this quiz, as in life, it's pretty easy for a Hollywood star to score.

The Too-Hard Basket

I should have known it was too good to be true. Standing at the ironing board at around 10.00 p.m., while Jocasta sprayed unspeakable chemicals at the shower recess, I finally spotted the white plastic bottom of the ironing basket.

It was quite a surprise, coming across it like this, after so many years. A door opened; an opportunity beckoned. I was one spotty shirt off achieving the unthinkable: a household in which there was no ironing waiting to be done.

Teenagers may have different fantasies, but later it comes down to this: that, just once, you could iron *everything*. But the fantasy goes further, gets wilder. If you could just defeat the ironing, you tell yourself, the rest of your domestic life might somehow slot back into control. You'd be organised. You'd be triumphant. Master of the Recycling Pile. Controller of Shower-Stall Scunge. Lord of all Toilet Ducks.

Of course, tomorrow there'll be more ironing, great straggling piles of it, heaved in off the line. But for one night, tonight, it will disappear — the stack of laundry baskets, perched one atop the other, that tottering mountain of reproach.

It's not only the washing which seems ready to engulf us. In the modern household, Chaos always seems to lurk about the porch, just waiting for its chance to invade. In the 21st-century household — a couple of incomes, a couple of kids, everything mortgaged to the hilt — the aim each week is merely to crawl across the line.

It's Saturday morning. The children haven't been arrested. Everyone's been fed something. There have been no major outbreaks of disease. The whole family's done a fantastic job.

But if you miss a single household job — if you lose attention just for a night — the whole edifice will surely come tumbling down. You'll be catapulted into the land of the Midnight Iron. Suddenly, Chaos will be on top of you, holding you down while you're kicking and wriggling on the ground. The margarine will have run out; the gas company will have cut off all supplies; stacks of ironing will be blocking all exits.

And Jocasta, defeated, will spend her evenings staring maniacally at the juice-stained couch. (Vainly does she threaten it with a pump-pack of fabric cleaner long since run dry.)

And so, to recover from our pathetic state, we must stay up late. Make an effort. Get Chaos back outside the door. Which is why we held the special extension to this Tuesday's Festival of the Iron (held concurrently with the weekly Adoration of the Bathroom).

Somewhere around 10.00 p.m., I find myself tackling Jocasta's spotty shirt. I'm taking my time with it, flicking the iron over it with an insouciant flourish. I'm looking forward to the moment when I march into the bathroom and hook the empty basket towards Jocasta, proclaiming my triumph with a thumping of my chest. *All three ironing baskets emptied!* Her very own Iron Man.

Then it happens. No, not an exploding iron. No, not a shirt that turns out to be rayon and bursts into flames. Defeat wears more mundane colours.

Jocasta, cleaning out the laundry, discovers we don't actually have three ironing baskets. We have *four*. And this one's been sitting around full for months. She walks in with it, and plonks it beside the ironing board, just as I complete the spotty shirt.

We all know what a left-to-last basket contains, don't we? It's the basket full of hard-to-iron items. Items sneaked in when your partner wasn't watching — a whole basket of pirate shirts, flounced frocks, delicate fabrics, pintucks, pleats, and ruched collars.

It's the Ironing Basket of Death. It's the Too-Hard Basket.

Perhaps you enjoy the bold, sweeping satisfaction of ironing a tea towel? Forget it. The ease of a handkerchief? Well, not in this lot. And so, nearing midnight, we sadly record a defeat, and slump back into the arms of Chaos.

But not for long. We shall regroup, our family. We shall be courageous. And then, without exactly telling her what's in it, we'll try to talk Jocasta's mother into tackling the Ironing Basket of Death.

Trying to stay afloat in the 21st century, you can't play every battle by the rules.

6

Add the pretentious literary references, and it seems clear that Jocasta thought she was getting some sort of fey intellectual with a cleaning fetish. Which must have been a shock when I finally moved in with my six weeks of dirty laundry, a Honda step-through motorcycle and the home-brew kit.

Competitive
Whingeing

Jocasta says she hopes I never cut my own leg off with a chainsaw because, if I do, she won't be taking any notice. She'll just be sitting inside, getting on with her First Aid by Correspondence course, ignoring the spurting blood and my frantic screams of 'Omigod, quick, quick — I think I'm dying.'

According to Jocasta, I've only myself to blame. Once too often, she says, she's heard me scream with an intensity that suggests the loss of at least one major body part, only to find me nursing a stubbed toe.

I explain to her that the pain is actually enormous — probably even worse than you'd get with a chainsaw and its nice clean cut. Then she rolls her eyes and heads back inside — presumably to add to her course notes on the topic of delusional dickheads. This makes me feel terrible. There's nothing worse than playing for sympathy, and finding your audience has left before interval.

Anyone can be a brave little soldier, but some of us believe our partner has the right to be absolutely familiar with the extent of our distress. Which is considerable. And getting worse.

Before you're partnered-up, you imagine the main things you'll want from a spouse are love, friendship, income and sex. But, after a few years together, you realise these are nothing compared to the ultimate gift a spouse can give: a good hour listening to you whinge.

Sex may dwindle, but this is something we get hot for every night. Right there on the doorstep, when you both come home and share a well-decanted whine. Not just a stubbed toe. But a mean boss, and a crowded train, and a bad-tempered client.

You tell your partner how unlucky you've been. How put upon. How unfortunate. And the good partner always sighs, and says: 'How horrible' and 'Poor you'.

It's not love. It's pity. And what a sweet prize it is.

When people are just getting together, they can't risk such scenes. They might share sex, but they never take turns in a good whinge.

You can see it in the advertisements in the singles columns. When people are trying to win a partner, they advertise themselves as having a perfect life. They are lucky, strong, happy. And — in bafflingly large numbers — they are windsurfers.

After a few years of marriage, we can be more honest. We can share just how rotten we feel. There's still the exaggeration you see in the singles ads, but now the exaggeration is running in the opposite direction. We want our partners to know what *losers* we are. We want our partners to know what a *bad catch* we have proved to be.

You can imagine if you summed up that nightly whinge in one of those singles ads:

Mr 40: Dead-tired man, sleeps badly, fed up with constant asthma attacks, did his back in moving the fridge, hates his boss and can hardly walk from the pain of an ingrowing toenail. Career, by the way, is at a dead end.

We can only thank God that he's found his perfect match in:

Ms 40: Put-upon woman, with wide variety of health problems, who missed the train today by 30 seconds. Her career is in crisis, she hates her own body, and her back is stuffed because her cheap husband won't buy a firmer bed.

We want someone to know how rough is our journey. Who else but our partner will share the descriptions of each bump and pothole?

The trick, of course, is to take turns — and get it over quickly. The hour before dinner is when most people do it. The not-so-happy hour, when everyone's tired and hungry and the indignities of the day are fresh in our minds.

It's a time for competitive whingeing, where both partners try to top the other's account of the horrors of the day. 'So you think *you've* had a bad day ...'; 'So you think *your* boss is a bastard ...'

It's that time of the day when all the world is four years old. And, best of all, you might even have some real four-year-olds there, adding to the melee — giving you the chance to tell them to 'Shut up and act your age.' It's still *daddy's* turn at the attention-seeking behaviour.

Then, when the real children are in bed, you can grow up yourselves, and start being adults together — warm and secure in the sweet embrace of your partner's abiding pity.

The Straights Mardi Gras

It's time for Australia's Annual Straights and Squares Mardi Gras, and what a great turnout it is — parading up the main street of your suburb. Let's see if we can spot some of the floats.

People in Elastic-Waisted Pants

They're back! This is the support group for heterosexual men and women who prefer clothing that has a bit of *give*, especially in the waist department. 'For too long our clothes have been in the closet — particularly my trackie daks and sloppy joes', says club president Amanda of Five Dock. 'Now, thanks to PEP, I'm letting comfort be my guide, even at work — whatever the hurtful comments of the fashion Nazis. Liberating? You bet!'

For the float, Amanda has once again arranged a spectacular display of loose-fitting leisure wear —

much of it with elastic expanders stitched into the sides.

A radical fringe of the group has refused to march, however, citing concerns about what's being left locked in the closet. 'Ugh Boots, for instance,' said a spokesman.

Blokes Who Prefer to be Taciturn

Societal pressure is a terrible thing — especially when every popular magazine is insisting that blokes open up and express their feelings. But what of those who were born taciturn and tongue-tied? Admits Ellen, the wife of one member: 'It's been hard to set up a political movement on behalf of Australia's taciturn blokes, as no-one ever wants to be spokesman.'

Club meetings, she says, tend to be fairly quiet affairs. 'A few years ago, they had a bit of a problem when Michael started to talk about his hostile feelings towards his father, but the rest of the guys just stared nervously at the floor, and Mike soon came to his senses. Ever since, it's been great.'

Simplicity is the mark of this float: just five blokes sitting on the back of a flat-top truck, keeping their own counsel, and taking occasional sips of beer. Would they like to see more respect for taciturn men? The men shift awkwardly from foot to foot: 'Oh, it's no big deal, but, yeah, that would be alright.'

The Knitting Nannas

A radical group of elderly knitters from Box Hill, all of whom openly share needles. The float is preceded by a marching band of young grandchildren, all wearing Aran jumpers with three arms.

Men Who Build Verandas

This is a group of men from Adelaide's south west who finds personal self-expression by building onto their homes. A rumpus room, a bloody huge barbecue, or a new veranda. 'We know it's daggy — but we don't give a stuff,' says the float's banner. Don't expect the TV cameras to get too close to *this* float. Each man has plastered it with a close-up photo of their latest veranda. 'It's great,' says one, 'to get out here and finally compare the size of our decks.'

Kids Who've Been Sucked Into Consumerism

'We try not to feel like we're victims,' says organiser Luke, aged seven, of Hobart, 'but we know we are.' Imagine it yourself: eating McDonalds, watching cable TV and playing Nintendo. What sort of life is that? 'And yet,' admits Luke, 'we find ourselves wanting it.' Whatever happened to the old pleasures — playing cricket, or riding a bike? Says Luke: 'Tonight we're going to reclaim them, riding ahead of the parade on a phalanx of old-fashioned bicycles.'

Organisers believe the group's name, Tykes on Bikes, is sure to catch on.

People Who Have a Good Laugh Over the Food and Style Sections of the Newspaper

'Mate, for us, the whole thing is just a scream,' says organiser Dennis, of Perth. 'I mean, people paying $32 for a steak! Bottles of wine for $25! And haircuts for blokes costing $70. The other day I saw an advert for a frypan costing $320.' Dennis's eyes start to water with mirth at the memory, the tears rolling down his face. 'I know it's rotten to laugh at minorities, but we do get some innocent pleasure from the style-setters.'

Dennis's float features a large freezer full of budget-priced meats, and late in the parade he's hoping to meet up with the Blokes Who Build Barbecues. The result should be just like the party at the end of the other Mardi Gras: absolutely sizzling.

Charm Offensive

'Remember', says Jocasta at the Parent–Teacher night, 'I'm counting on you to break his spirit. That's why we pay our taxes; for exactly this sort of professional help.'

The Space Cadet's teacher grimaces. 'I do *try* to break his spirit,' she says. 'But every time I crush a little bit of it, another bit pops up.'

The Space Cadet has been born with rather too much personal charm. Too much of a cheeky smile. It worries me. Out in the playground, some Year Six girls are carrying The Space Cadet around as if he's something between a small deity and a stuffed toy. He giggles, wriggles loose from their arms, and runs in fast circles around them.

I hear Jocasta, plotting with the teacher, suggesting various methods to crush his spirit. 'He's so cute,' chorus the girls outside. Whatever Jocasta and the teacher come up with, I get the feeling it won't be much of an antidote to this.

I don't know how to deal with The Space Cadet: I was always an ungainly and ugly child. I wonder whether it wasn't a better start in life.

When I was a baby my ears stuck out so badly my mother decided to Sellotape them down in the hope of changing the direction of their growth. The Gloved-One did this daily, first thing in the morning, plastering them down from several angles like a difficult-to-wrap package.

She did this right up until the district nurse visited and suggested it might be the cause of the bright red rash that suddenly had broken out, right around my skull.

Anyways, between the bright red rash and the bounced-back ears there weren't a lot of people crowding around my pram. Tough at the time perhaps. But at least I didn't develop any early illusions about life. Now, of course, the rash has long died down, I have a balanced attitude about my attractiveness to others, and my ears are relatively flat. ('*That's* because of the Sellotaping,' points out my mother, pretty much whenever I see her.)

I wonder if this isn't the answer with The Space Cadet. We could make it a family tradition, and Sellotape his ears to make them stick out. At least he'd have something to worry about.

A friend says that when his two daughters are in their late adolescence, he'll be happy for them to be escorted out by Batboy, who, he is convinced, will drive carefully and return them home on time. He'd like it to be known, right now, that calls from The Space Cadet will not be received — rather too much blond hair; too much of a glint in the eye. The need to crush his spirit becomes a yet more urgent task.

By the time of my adolescence, my mother had given up on the ears, and was focusing on the teeth. This time she sought professional help, and consulted an orthodontist. (Sellotape would have gone limp in the mouth.)

After enduring braces for two years, I removed the whole $2 000 contraption, in one my rare displays of adolescent defiance. Out in the shed one desperate afternoon, I did the deed, loosening the glue using a chisel, a hammer and a pair of pliers.

From memory I had a date that night, and had decided my hoped-for girlfriend might not like kissing me with my braces. (As opposed to the bleeding, chisel-chipped gums and glue-stained teeth with which I instead presented her.)

In a neat parallel to the Sellotape affair, it soon became obvious I'd removed the braces about a year too soon. More patience, and today I'd be Brad Pitt.

I wonder about The Space Cadet. What if the teachers can't break his spirit? Is there anyone who could perform a bit of reverse orthodontics?

Back in the playground, The Space Cadet is standing on the library steps, dancing and waving at the Year Six girls. 'Come and get me,' he shouts, before running, hands outstretched, straight towards them.

A set of buck teeth, to match his dad's? It may be our only hope.

The Milk-Crate Couch

It has come to this: standing with Jocasta looking at curtain fabrics, attempting to be proper grown-ups. Suddenly, under this sort of pressure, I have a rush of nostalgia. This fifteen-bucks-a-metre curtain fabric is all very well, but what of the decorating I used to do in my early twenties? The decorating that is still practised with such flamboyance by young blokes everywhere.

We know about the Bauhaus movement, the minimalists, and the Federation style. But has anyone thought to record that unique, indigenous style? That school of decorating we could, with pride, call 'Australian young guy'.

Surely now is the time.

Furniture

The fans of the Australian vernacular are already buying up the nation's Laminex tables and bright orange lamps. How much longer before the antique shops feature that other rustic creation of the 1960s and '70s: the upside-down milk-crate couch? First developed by two Brisbane lads in the early '60s, it soon swept the nation. It was the soft southerners who added the piece of foam placed atop the four milk crates; and the Adelaide guys who, with their customary sense of style, added two more milk crates, placed opposite the couch, to provide a sort of conversation pit.

Later, some say from Darwin, came the idea of adding a coffee table — typically a casual, eclectic affair. Again the emphasis on the 'found object' — an upturned garbage bin, a wooden fruit box, an empty wine cask.

Which brings us to the scatter cushions. Having emptied the wine cask, one often found oneself in urgent need of a pillow. Only to find that God — or Berri Estates — had miraculously provided one, right there in the box. Over months, the resulting silver, blown-up wine-bladders bestowed an edge of night-club glamour to many a lounge room.

Add a bookshelf, made of teetering planks balanced on ill-matched bricks, and you'd have achieved something pretty close to 'The Look'.

Upholstery

In some houses the milk-crate couch was rendered unnecessary, due to the possession of an old settee, usually losing its stuffing. Would the young guys spend $2 000 having it recovered in a fine damask? Well, no. I once lived in a house in Brisbane in which one of the great innovations occurred. My memory is that it was a fellow called Marcus who first had the idea; his clarity of vision still cannot fail to impress.

Faced with a worn-out couch, Marcus visited the local auto-care centre, and invested $20 in a stretchy Holden car-seat cover. It took us a while to fit it over our old couch, pulling it down over the back, tying it around the bottom, and cutting it in around the armrest. But for months it conferred upon the flat all the sophistication of an international motor show.

Floor Coverings

On the floor? Not so much throw rugs, as *thrown* rugs — bits of carpet chucked away by the neighbours. But still good for soaking up the oil from the half-dismantled Kawasaki motorbike taking pride of place in the middle of the floor.

Posters

Position! Position! Position! People often used to comment on our poster positioning: it was certainly eclectic. One poster in the corner of the room, right up near the ceiling. A second right down near the floor, beside the kitchen cupboards. Was it designed to create a sense of space and freedom? No, it was designed to hide the two spots where serious mould had broken out.

Indeed, occasionally the poster of Elvis used to positively glisten with moisture, much along the lines of the weeping Madonnas of southern Italy. For what did Elvis weep? Well, probably for the general standard of food preparation and hygiene.

In *this* house, not only did all our T-shirts say 'support wildlife', they actually did it.

Curtaining, etc.

For curtaining, we usually opted for the flannelette sheet thumb-tacked to the architrave; while a 'lived-in' feel was happily provided by the empty pizza boxes gaily scattered about the floor.

Back in the curtain shop, Jocasta and I are torn between plaid and the textured linen. We are aware of the problem: we have too little good taste to choose well; but just enough to realise, once the credit card leaves our hand, that we'll have made a shocking mistake.

We'll have to borrow some young guy's milk-crate couch, put our feet up, and have a good hard think.

Hard Yards

My father-in-law stands at the back door, and shakes his head. Like all persons over sixty he knows about gardens, about mulch, about fertilisers. He examines the devastation before he speaks. 'But you must have realised it would be a disaster,' is all he says.

From the faraway look in his eyes, it seems he's finally aware of the very murky genetic pool into which his daughter has leapt.

Together, we stare at the strange patterns on the grass: a sharply drawn circle of dead grass, cross-hatched with tall sprigs of luminous green. The whole backyard looks like a painting by Kandinsky — full of weird squiggles and semicircles of dead grass.

'I mean, it's not hard,' my father-in-law adds. 'The instructions are on the packet. Did you read the packet?'

I shift a little from foot to foot. 'No,' I say, 'I didn't read the packet.'

'Humph', says my father-in-law, with a small self-satisfied smile. 'Well, I *always* read the packet.'

I find myself wondering if my father-in-law, if properly composted, could be turned into a useful sort of mulch.

This is one of the things about men who are over sixty. For years, they operated on the ancient male principle of reading the instructions only when all else has failed. Now, tragically, their testosterone levels have rapidly dropped. Right down to a level where they may be in danger of behaving sensibly.

I finally say: 'What I did was to take a guess at it.' The guess, in this case, was that you should pour half a pack of lawn fertiliser into a single watering can, before searching around the house for the rose that fits on the end of the can, then, having failed to find it, decide to do the job anyway.

'I just figured,' I say to my father-in-law, 'that if I sort of danced about, letting the watering can spin around, then it would sort of splash out evenly.'

It was at this point that my father-in-law rolled his eyes. Thus turning any action I might take against him into a quite defensible *crime passionnel*. Four years maximum sentence. With good behaviour, I could well be out by the Christmas after next. By which time, my *extra-nutritious* mulch would surely have solved all my gardening problems.

As far as I can see, there are only two or three options with lawn: you can fertilise it, and watch it die; or leave it to Mother Nature, and watch it die.

Or, alternatively, you could attack your over-critical father-in-law with an axe and, two months later, ensconced in your cell with three over-friendly Tongans, find that lawn care is no longer foremost in your mind.

It's the same story with the compost heap, which, my father-in-law says, if properly built, will not smell. And so I've built the whole thing to his instructions, only to discover that the reason it doesn't smell is the army of mice who eat everything before it's had the chance to rot.

I consider offering some tart criticisms, but by now he's wandered off. He's walking around the lawn, following the trail of the of the luminous, long grass growing in lines where my over-strength fertiliser slopped from the watering can.

Unluckily for me, he's moved into his amused mode. 'Actually, one could plot your progress,' he says, matching his feet to the patches of green. 'It's like the steps of a dance. Recorded in the grass.'

At this point, my father-in-law begins performing a lunatic's dance on the lawn, tracing my steps, flinging his hands in the air, letting his head loll from side to side. He prances about, occasionally throwing his head back to laugh at my expense. Watching him, I no longer want to mulch my father-in-law. Submerged in concrete, and then turned out to dry, he'd actually make a most striking garden gnome.

He leaps high, his feet spinning in the air, landing on either side of the green stripes.

I consider his past advice. At considerable effort I put in a garden pool (result: massive increase in mosquitoes). I put in a large tree (result: massive increase in leaves dumped on lawn). And I put in a rockery (result: massive increase in trips to the nursery after all the plants die).

Why, considering this, do I feel so inadequate next to the old boy, just because he can throw around terms such as top-dressing and aeration? Finally, I approach him.

'I know I'm a dope,' I offer.

'Not at all,' he says, throwing a paternal arm around my shoulder. 'I don't understand you young blokes. You don't seem to understand that gardening is boring. In my day, we'd have just concreted the bastard over.'

OK. Sure. Now, finally, I will *have* to kill him.

Letterbug

When I went on holidays, I told my colleague, Tony Squires, to open all my mail. 'Everything, mate,' I said grandly. 'Don't worry if it says "private" on the envelope or anything; it might be something urgent.' This — and I mention it in case you ever consider issuing such an invitation yourself — was a staggeringly stupid mistake.

I got back after holidays to find Squires dancing up and down the corridor, waving a handwritten letter and guffawing merrily. 'It seemed a bit personal so I didn't read past the first page,' he lied.

He thrust the thing into my hand and instantly the full horror was revealed. It was a love letter. Worse. It was written by me. When I was fifteen. And it ended by quoting large slabs of Kahlil Gibran.

The woman, who'd received my letter twenty-five years before, had — with perfect timing — chosen this moment to uncover it during her house-move and post it straight into the welcoming hands of Mr Squires. That same Mr Squires who, a full two weeks later, can't pass me in the corridor without his lips tightening into a small, suppressed smile.

Of course, in Newcastle, where Squires grew up, they don't have love letters; it's just a matter of a quick feel-up in the back of dad's Commodore. But, for the rest of us, the adolescent love letter remains a uniquely embarrassing literary form.

How embarrassing? Ah, let me count the ways.

Borrowed Verse

All teenage love letters have some borrowed verse, and it's nearly always one of the same three poems: the lofty thing from Andrew Marvell, the hippie thing from Kahlil Gibran, and the slightly sexy thing from e. e. cummings. Indeed, my letter may provide some sort of record in including all three. (Which is one up on Mr Squires, who presumably did his serenading armed with a copy of *Limericks Lewd and Lusty*.)

Margin Art

If it doesn't contain a poorly executed attempt at artwork, then it's not a real teenage love letter. Mine, for instance, contains a very colourful, and almost unrecognisable, attempt at a field of daisies — which alone may explain why the recipient of the letter has taken twenty-five years to contact me again. Would I have done better with two intertwined hearts? With a geometric? With an AC/DC logo? These questions torment me still.

Political/Philosophical Chat

It's always important to include a few slogans in your letter, just to dignify the whole process. Mine, for instance, contains some pretty tough political comments about Malcolm Fraser. Indeed, some sort of discussion about how The Dismissal was engineered by 'you know, real fascists' was the precursor to nearly all my teenage snog sessions — so much so that the mere mention of Malcolm Fraser's name still gives me a small erotic charge.

Pathetic Attempts at Grown-Up talk

This is a must. You may be fifteen years old, and so may she — but there's no need to admit it. What you need is a pathetic and obvious attempt to talk like a grown-up. I can see I'm going to be forced to quote a slab of my letter, to show you what I mean. Thus: 'Woke up this morning at the god-awful sonavabitch time of 6 o'clock, so I am at this moment sitting in the school canteen trying to resurrect myself with hot chocolate.'

It is, if I say so myself, a superb example of the form — the Clint Eastwood tough-talk of 'sonavabitch' rubbing up so disastrously with the truthful admission of 'hot chockie'. Embarrassing? Oh, yes.

Actual Promises

These, I note, are completely missing in this early — and failed — attempt at winning love, but are present during my rather more successful wooing of Jocasta. Indeed, by Jocasta's time, my love-letter techniques had improved to include the bare-faced lie — in particular, at one clearly desperate point, the claim that I'd do half the housework if she'd only let me move in. Add the constant pretentious literary references, and it seems clear that Jocasta thought she was getting some sort of fey intellectual with a cleaning fetish.

(Which must have been a shock when I finally moved in with my six weeks of dirty laundry, a Honda step-through motorcycle and the home-brew kit.)

Déjà View

Most of us watch TV, and most have a sense of *déjà vu* when we're doing it. Have we seen it all before? Sure. Largely because all of TV is governed by a secret rule book.

1. Every office in sitcom America has a short, perky, libidinous red-head with kooky clothes and no apparent job.
2. Any injury whatsoever to a Jehovah's Witness will require a blood transfusion.
3. Minor characters in TV drama, despite appearing weekly over a number of years, never get a change of clothes.
4. Supermarket shopping, carried into the kitchen, only ever consists of one bag. It never contains toilet paper.
5. Every square metre of Sydney Harbour has at least a couple of floating bodies. Watching *Water Rats*, it's a miracle they still manage to get the ferries through to Manly.
6. The judges who preside over cases in the United States are always African–American.

7. Being the sibling of a police officer or a doctor is pretty much asking for it: I'd give it three episodes before you're revealed as a heroin addict.

8. The main guy's an Anglo; the sidekick is from a minority group.

9. The main guy is handsome; the sidekick is both fatter and shorter.

10. The circled classified ad left by the murderer is always in the middle of the page of classifieds, never on the top or side.

11. Only on game shows does the carry-over champ win $61 000 of prizes — which works out as one pin-ball machine and three nights on Hamilton Island. Remind me to never shop where they shop.

12. Radio announcers, heard for three seconds through the car radio, just happen to be conveniently announcing both the time and place of the scene: 'And it's a beautiful morning in Adelaide.'

13. Criminals never shop at Target. That fibre fragment discovered at the crime scene comes from a jacket that could only be bought at a single shop in southern Glasgow, during the years 1951 to 1953.

14. Heroin use leads to an inability to shave.

15. Everyone in New York can see the Manhattan skyline out their window, just as every single citizen of Sydney has a view of the Sydney Harbour Bridge.

16. As people glide through the airport, no suitcase ever looks as heavy as a real one.

17. The only compatible organ donor is the no-good, long-lost father.

18. The policeman at the crime scene is always starting a fresh notebook.

19. The crucial phone message left by the kidnapper is always the first on the message tape ... the audience conveniently spared the four messages from the video shop.

20. Everyone pulls up right outside their venue, and finds a parking spot, even in the middle of New York.

21. Murderers have long tired of simply shooting people. Not when they could have fun with mirrored walls, electrical spikes, and trampolines buried in lawns.

22. The big boss is always a humourless, thin-lipped stickler for the rules, handling pressure from above.

23. The more brilliant and intuitive the cop, the worse his bad breath/rumpled clothes/psycho-sexual problems.

24. And, most curious of all, beautiful young women always, and inexplicably, fall for craggy older guys.

7

My favourite was the cover headline: 'Small Breasts are Back in Fashion'. And you were left wondering: what does the editor imagine? That women like Jocasta have sets of these things? That they get up every morning, umming and ahhing about whether they'll slide on the 38 double-Ds or the 32 As?

Daddy Longer Legs

Jocasta is trying to get me out of bed, employing the customary method of throwing the kids in there with me, using them like small incendiaries. It's certainly a terrifying scene, and one that normally brings a rapid end to the Reading of the Newspaper. But not this morning.

However much the kids wriggle, I can't take my eyes off the bold headline in the free magazine. It's on the fashion page, in the same type they normally use to announce that 'Spring Dresses will be Shorter' or 'Winter Coats are Darker'. Except this time it says, and I am not making this up, 'Summer Legs are Longer'.

Lying in bed, with my string-tie pyjamas cutting into my growing roll of fat, with last night's Mudgee red still pounding just behind the eyeballs, and with two children bouncing up and down on my ribs, I wonder just how I am meant to use this information.

Already, the fashion industry seems to have totally removed women's secondary sexual characteristics. The sexy arse ('the Lopez') is, of course, long gone; and even the breast is a fading memory. (In the latest designs, it is finally uncovered — but only in order that we may note its virtual disappearance.)

It's only a theory, but with every passing day the fashion models are getting thinner while I am getting fatter. There's good evidence, I now believe, that Eva Herzigova is channelling her buttocks onto mine — rather in the way that Lake George, just outside Canberra, rises and falls according to rain levels in Western Australia. Every time *she* eats a hamburger, I put on two kilos.

And now this. 'Summer Legs are Longer'. Clearly, in order to be fashionable, I'll have to make mine grow. But how?

Already, the fashion industry demands its brutal entry price. For the women, starving yourself until you are a celery-stick off death, then surgically gouging any loose skin from your face. And now the ultimate: demanding we strive for longer limbs, presumably by being stretched on some sort of medieval rack. The fashion industry may be swinging away from the torture of animals, but not from the torture of its own customers.

Back in the bed, I am sweating slightly, lost in my nightmare, while Batboy mutters to his brother, explaining how to use one's father as a trampoline.

I ignore them and show Jocasta the headline, hoping to share the horror, but she says I'm being stupid — they mean summer legs will *look* longer because of the different clothes.

Of course, she's the one being naive. Lots of ideas from the fashion industry have sounded stupid, but that hasn't stopped them. For instance: the trend of getting fuller lips — achieved by having fat suctioned off your bum and injected into your lips. Who would have believed that a few years ago? Or believed that, in the 21st century, when a group of style-setters smother each other with kisses, they are literally kissing each other's arses?

Then there's my personal favourite, the cover headline that announced in huge print: 'Small Breasts are Back in Fashion'.

What a great headline it was — a really practical fashion tip for all those readers confused about what size breasts to choose. You were really left wondering: what does the editor imagine? That women like Jocasta have sets of these things, just sitting there in the wardrobe? That they get up every morning and stand in front of their mirrors, umming and ahhing about whether they'll slide on the 38 double-Ds or the 32 As?

Or that reading their magazines, they'll let out a whoop of excitement: 'Oh, thank God I didn't throw out those squitchy little ones back in 1982. I just knew they'd come back.'

Out at the Royal Easter Show a while ago, my friend Jennifer was staring at the signs outside the funfair ride. Each ride had a masonite cut-out of a little boy, and a sign: 'If you are not as tall as me, you can't come on this ride.'

Jennifer reckons city dress shops might as well go the same way. Outside each store they'd be a masonite depiction of a model: 'If your waist isn't as thin as mine, I wouldn't bother.' They could even have a cut-out in the doorway: to get in the door, you have to be able to squeeze through.

Which store will you be able to enter? Which size breasts should you choose? And what length legs would be right for me?

I lie there distracted, as Batboy begins his climb on to the bedhead, ready to perform the dive-bomb on my belly, shouting to The Space Cadet to move aside.

Finally Jocasta has had enough of my blubbering. She grabs my ankles, heaving me out of bed just as Batboy launches his dive-bomb. There's an ominous crack but I'm sure my legs are longer.

My body destroyed? Of course, but fashionably so.

We Cook, You Praise

'All I need to know is how much olive oil to put in the mix,' I say to Jocasta, 'and then you come in and try to highjack the whole operation.' I wave an egg flip towards her in a vaguely intimidating way.

'Well,' says Jocasta, 'if you don't want my advice, I'll just leave you to stew in your own juices. Over-oiled though they may be.'

She shoots the fish a look of commiseration, as if she wished its life had not been so clearly in vain, and marches from the kitchen. This is the problem with Jocasta: too often she does exactly what I ask. In this case, leaving me alone in the kitchen with a rather threatening piece of fish and no recipe.

What Jocasta doesn't understand is that, in the kitchen, I want exactly the *right* amount of advice. Enough to make the meal edible — and to prevent any outbreaks of disease — but not so much advice that I'll have to share any resulting glory. If the guests love it, no way do I want to find myself forced to mumble it was all down to her recipe.

Women claim to know plenty about cooking, but still they seem ignorant about that special culinary area: Bloke's Cooking. Maybe some guidance would help.

Rule 1: We do it for the glory

Forget the 'special delight of providing nourishment'. Forget 'the quiet warmth of watching people eat'. That's girls' stuff. Blokes want feedback. Lots of it. Women's cookbooks may display Expected Preparation Time; the blokes' edition instead lists Expected Praise and Adoration (expressed in hours). After the basting, in other words, should always come the basking.

And luckily we're happy to help, with a series of subtle, after-dinner, conversation starters, including:
- 'Go on, everybody, say it, I've overcooked the meat.'
- 'Does anybody else think I've hideously overdone the *nuoc mam*?'

Or, on occasions where the meal is actually awful:
- 'It's certainly a bit dry; I think Jocasta's going to have to change that recipe of hers.'

Rule 2: The greater the mess, the better the meal

Others can cook the hum-drum, everyday meals. (For instance: women.) We prefer something that's a bit of a challenge, something with a degree of difficulty, something, in other words, totally beyond our ability. Which is why we choose the most show-offy, fancy-pants recipes in the book. Recipes that involve Tahitian spices, bundt tins, and obscure German sweetmeats.

Not only do such recipes lend themselves to lengthy discussion afterwards; they also turn your kitchen into a vivid monument to each stage of the bloke's heroic struggle — filth, mess and unwashed pots covering every surface. Remember the basic rule of Bloke's Cooking: no real meal has been produced in this kitchen before. Nor, it seems, will be again.

Rule 3: The more ingredients, the better the meal

There is no requirement, under the rules of Bloke's Cooking, to use ingredients economically. By the end of your preparation, the place should be full of half-cut lemons, open packets left to go stale, and cheeses left out of the fridge. Remember: you're an *artist*.

Rule 4: When in doubt, barbecue

It's outside, it involves dead animals, and it's dangerous. (Particularly once you and your mates are onto the second cask, and Mark suggests a bit more oomph via the lawnmower fuel.)

Rule 5: Men's cooking is exempt from any need to be balanced or nutritious

That's right: a bloke's meal is so special and fabulous it can't be judged by such narrow parameters as nutrition. Any passing woman can make the salad; he's too busy creating the home-made pizza with triple cheese and extra oil. Expected praise: Five Days.

Rule 6: Don't expect the kids to eat before midnight

This is our one confession. Blokes make fabulous cooks: flamboyant, emotional and vocal. But we have been known to stuff up the timing. Indeed, the expectation that artists like us should be kept to some sort of suburban timetable is just a little bit offensive.

Besides, even if the meal ends before midnight, it's not as if the diners can leave straight away. There's the meal to discuss. 'Come on, admit it, I overdid the *tabia lombok*, didn't I?'

Fields of Dreams

'People said you were a rotten team,' says Batboy's soccer coach, Sam, addressing the boys in his usual Churchillian style. The boys are all exhausted, sucking at oranges, but they're listening hard. Sam — who's Italian, and knows the value of a rhetorical flourish — pauses for effect and then stabs at the air with his hand. 'Well, anyone who says that you're a rotten team now, well, they'd have to have rocks in their head.'

Eleven-year-old boys don't give a lot away, but I can see them quietly glancing at each other, out from under their fringes, a clamped-down smile creeping onto their faces. They know something transforming has happened to them, somewhere in the last four months.

Sam doesn't go into details, because we all know the story. The long season last year when Batboy's team didn't win a single game. OK, let's be honest here, didn't score a single *goal*. Not one. Not even close. All season. Not even against teams which could only field eight players. Not even against the team whose goalie was bored, fiddling with the net, and got himself tangled, unable to move. Not even then.

The boys coped fine with their losses, although they

did develop a sudden taste for American sports films — and always with the same plot. A team that couldn't score a single goal or point, a team which everyone laughed at, miraculously came good. They could watch that plot a thousand times. Especially on Saturday afternoons, following that week's crushing defeat.

This season, Batboy found himself in a team made up of remnants of various old teams. Few knew each other, and they had sharply different temperaments. Quickly they fell into warring factions. There was even the odd punch being thrown. It was a spiky group of kids, one that didn't look likely ever to play together as a team.

I was remembering how grim things seemed at the beginning of this season, as I stood watching Sam finish his speech. 'You didn't win today,' he tells the boys, 'but you played great football. You showed character.'

This is Sam's favourite word, so he says it again: 'Character.' He points to David, his co-coach. 'We didn't do it,' he says, 'we just coached you. You guys did it. You did it for yourselves. You found out what happens when you play like a team.'

Sam makes the *best* speeches. By the end of it, the boys are dazed, drunk on praise, and various parents are dabbing at their eyes with tissues.

Sam pauses for effect again, and tells them they've made the semifinals. We're going to have extra practice for the next few weeks. He reckons they might even be in with a chance.

I look out over the neighbouring ovals, and see other teams dotted around, all with their coaches and their managers. Lots of little speeches. Lots of emotion. Lots of lessons. And yet none of it seems to fit into the public discourse that we have about ourselves. We talk also about how society has fragmented, how there's no community left, yet to believe all that, is to squeeze our eyes shut to this — these people, on every oval in every city and town.

Sam and David are young guys, without kids of their own yet. Both soccer mad. When Sam finishes his speech, someone tells the boys it's his birthday, and so they crowd around and sing to him, laughing to see their coach blush and stumble. They slap their arms around each other, and babble about the semis. They're a team.

One week later they win the semi, and then — with a penalty shoot-out — the final. Another week on and it's the grand final.

Tino — one of Sam and David's friends — leans towards me, and whispers conspiratorially. 'We've heard Burwood has come up with a new formation. They're going to try to surprise us on Saturday.'

I pass the information to Batboy, and a flicker of fear crosses his face. 'But, Dad, what do you think they'll try to do?' Batboy's not used to talk of soccer strategy. To him, the word 'formation' has only one implication, and that's military.

I explain: 'It's just a new way of placing their players. They'll be trying to come up with an answer to "*Il Pressing*".' He nods. Of course. Burwood would be *desperate* to find an answer to '*Il Pressing*'.

'*Il Pressing*' is our coaches' secret weapon. It's what's taken Batboy's team from being awarded Most Pathetic in the Inner West, to today's moment of drama.

Already the boys chatter among themselves, dropping the term '*Il Pressing*' as if they've known it from birth.

'Well that's what you get with "*Il Pressing*",' I hear Jimmy say to Will, real casual.

Actually, it was only last week our Italian–Australian coaches confessed they've had a particular strategy all year — one based, and I swear I'm not making this up, on that used by the Dutch National Team in the 1974 World Cup. 'Total football'. Or, in the Italian, '*Il Pressing*'.

I've watched Sam and David, arguing about it with Tino and Maria; all four bent over David's chalkboard, arrows flying everywhere, diagrams more complex than for the Battle of Waterloo. And all directed at the second-lowest division of the Under–11 competition, in a single corner of an Australian city. Such arguments! Such knowledge! Such history!

Tino stares at the chalkboard and announces that '*Il Pressing*' is too dangerous. David points out that after the Dutch let it go, it was taken up by the Italian national side. He squares his shoulders and emphasises his point: 'The Italians — the most technically-correct soccer nation of all time.'

What can Tino do? He's hardly going to disagree. So '*Il Pressing*' it is.

But when Sam drags the boys together, he doesn't talk to them about winning. It's another of his Churchillian speeches. 'It's not about winning. It's not even about soccer. You got here not because of your soccer. Not because you kick well.'

I notice how he steps around using the words 'win' and 'lose'. 'You got here because you played like a team; because you had respect for each other; because you showed character.'

Sam's been to the laminator, and he hands them bits of laminated cardboard, telling them to pin them next to their beds. It says: 'A champion team is remembered longer than a team of champions.'

Already that week, before the tension of the grand final, Sam had handed out the photocopied yearbook. It had pages of little paragraphs: each coach's assessment of each boy and girl. We'd all read what the coaches had written about our team. James, they'd written, is 'the true definition of an Italian striker.' Young Nicholas a 'typical Italian-style attacker.' Fast Edward is like Maradonna. Evan plays 'in the true modern way, à la Paolo Maldini.'

And Batboy — since you ask — is the spitting image of Gaetano Scirea.

It's 10.30 on a late winter morning, and they are about to run out for the Grand Final. This gaggle of ordinary boys, straggling over the field, but in their coach's eyes, each holding hands with one of the greats.

So much has been written about the darkness of our culture. But there is also this. Coaches who see greatness in the most unlikely of materials; and children hungry for that transforming gift.

I see my boy holding his body a little differently, enjoying what it can do, the skills he's learnt, the confidence he's won from earning David and Sam's regard. There may be an answer to 'Il Pressing' — we'll find out today — but not, I think, to all the other things they have learnt.

Blackballed

There's an old dentist joke in which the dentist is leaning forward over the patient, about to start the drill, when the patient shifts forward and gets a pretty workable grip on the dentist's testicles. Says the patient: 'Let's agree not to hurt each other, OK?'

I was repeating this joke to myself, as a sort of dulling mantra, while sitting on the metal chair waiting for the doctor. I knew what was about to happen. This complete stranger — sure, he *claimed* to be a doctor — would soon invite me into his rooms, request I remove my pants, then give my knackers a good hard squeeze. If only I were armed with a dentist's drill, it might put things on a more equal footing.

Men are getting a lot of heat these days for our refusal to have regular check-ups at the doctor, but my experiences have not been good. For a start, amid the current blaze of litigation, doctors seem unwilling to do anything without a flurry of tests.

Walk into a Sydney surgery with a harpoon sticking out of your head, and the typical GP will start insisting on a blood test and an X-ray 'just so we can rule out prostate cancer'.

He'll then get quite shirty if you suggest the reason you feel unwell may be connected to this enormous harpoon, and the fact that buckets of blood are, as you speak, spurting forth from the wound. The implication is that he hasn't done six years of medical school to have patients telling him what a harpoon looks like.

'Well, usually we find the harpoon is masking deeper problems,' he'll say, gloomily gloving-up to commit a few passing indignities on one's bottom.

This time, I didn't even have something as complex as a harpoon injury. I'd presented to my GP with a good, straightforward injury, caused by dropping a double-hung sash window on my right foot — yet still ended up with a referral to a specialist to have my testicles squeezed.

Which is fine, except two weeks later I find myself sitting in the specialist's waiting room, and already I've been here for a full hour and a half, floridly imagining my galloping testicular cancer, while enduring a truly ancient copy of *Woman's Day*.

Specialists appear to have some sort of agreement that a patient must sit in the waiting room for at least two hours, presumably so one's heartbeat can return to normal after hearing the cost of the consultation.

Of course, as patients, we should stand up for our rights — making the same sort of fuss we'd make if kept waiting for an hour at a restaurant or a bar. The only difference being that, at the time he's listening to your complaint, the bartender usually doesn't have you on a table, stretched out naked, with his hands cupped around your balls.

Depending, of course, on your personal choice of bar.

Eventually, though, my doctor sauntered in, showed me to a side room and promptly left me for a further twenty minutes — no doubt so I could complete my galloping cancer fantasies — then returned and began the examination.

Which brings me to the other reason we blokes don't enjoy seeing doctors. Their use of the phrase 'Oh, my God.' For myself, I find the phrase 'Oh, my God' quite useful, especially after a trip to the hairdresser. It's less useful when uttered by a doctor who at that precise moment is examining my testicles.

Doc: 'Oh, my God.'

Me (voice a-quiver): 'What do you mean: "Oh, my God"?'

Doc (fascinated): 'It's the lump. It's huge!'

Me (showing the sort of dignity you'd expect): 'Awwwwwww! I'm dying!! Awwwwwwwwww!!!'

Doc (as if stating the bleeding obvious): 'Course, it's harmless, just a haematoma. But by God it's a big 'un.'

It's at this point he wanders out, no doubt to check his waiting room queue isn't moving too fast, leaving me to stumble out into Macquarie Street, wondering if those two hours reading *Woman's Day* might have done some permanent intellectual damage. Hope not. Otherwise I'll need another check-up.

The Kitchen Blues

The worst moment was on Old Windsor Road, with me driving along, Jocasta in the passenger seat, and each of us screaming about whether we should choose the *calypso* blue or the *china* blue. Of course, the colours are identical, but that wasn't going to stop an experienced married couple like us from enjoying a fairly extended argument.

Especially since I could picture just how superbly the calypso blue would set off the white kitchen appliances, while the china blue would drag us into a life of degradation, shame and frothing insanity. And if you'll give me a moment, I'll try to work out which colour is which.

That's what happens when you decide to fix up your kitchen; suddenly you find yourself thinking the colour of your benchtops is an issue of some importance, right up there with the changing role of NATO.

You find yourself speaking a language called 'Kitchen' — raving about coordinated trims and multi-function ovens with the intensity you once reserved for sex. It's Kitchen Lust, and it keeps you awake at nights — trailing your fingers over imagined whitegoods, wondering how long it will before you'll be alone together, just you and them, and how you'll get to turn them on.

But like all lust, Kitchen Lust brings its ghostly sibling, fear. You'll make a terrible mistake. You'll go all the way with the wrong colour. And you'll end up not with a kitchen, but a *kitsch*-en.

It's the kitchen outfitters who are to blame. They're the people trying to convince us that kitchens are important; that the world judges people according to the colour of their benchtops. 'Are you marble people or laminate people?' the saleswoman asked chirpily, right before she checked whether we were 'fawn people or bright colours people'.

And so Jocasta and I cheerily admitted we were laminate people *and* bright colours people, which, translated into the language of 'Kitchen', means roughly: 'Look, everyone, the Suburban Trash has arrived.'

Certainly, there's nothing like staring at a wall-full of laminate samples to make you feel it's all hopeless; that you'll end up with a colour combination proved to cause grand mal seizures in laboratory mice.

First up, there's the row of reds and coppers — sophisticated tones which can transform the most humble home into an up-market brothel. And there, just below, are the charming pastel blues and pinks — irresistible colours for anyone considering converting their kitchen into a Darrell Lea outlet.

But the more colour chips you accumulate — and I've so many I rattle when I walk — the more you realise you're about to do something both ghastly and permanent. That's the point about Jocasta and me. We know we've got bad taste. We've seen the clothes we buy.

And the mistakes I've made in the shirt department should look quite startling when seen over a whole benchtop.

That's why we've become so obsessed.

Witness the moment in the cinema — halfway through the climactic scene in Roddy Doyle's *The Snapper*. There was the father, berating his daughter for becoming pregnant; there was the tearful girl, passionately refusing to name the man responsible. And, somehow, by means of the hairs on my neck, I knew it. 'Are you,' I whispered to Jocasta, 'thinking the same thing as I am?'

'Yes', she admitted, her voice thick with emotion. 'Those cupboards in the foreground; I wonder if we could get handles like that.'

Now, of course, we're judging all films that way; as a sort of cinematic kitchen catalogue.

The scene in the gangster movie, where the villain smashes someone's head open against the kitchen cupboards? Sure it was ghastly — but did you see how easily the blood wiped off that Corian surface?

And what about the movie where the drug courier frantically tries to stuff his cannabis into an already packed kitchen drawer? At last we could feel good — we've ordered pot drawers *twice* that size.

When will our obsession end? Only when we've spent our thousands of dollars, stared for a week at our horrible choices, and then realised that no-one judges your personality on your kitchen anyway. They look through your record collection instead.

Now we *really* need to do some shopping.

Party Animal

I have come across the following scrawled notes lying on my own bedside table. I cannot think who they belong to, although the handwriting is somehow familiar.

I publish them in case the warnings they contain may be of use to others.

Notes to self after returning home from a party

I will henceforth begin with beer. And not with red wine. And certainly not with gin.

I will no longer make a pig of myself with the guacamole. I will especially refrain from polishing off a whole serve before the other guests arrive, noting my shame when Michelle felt it necessary to place her body between me and the access point to the second bowl.

When being introduced to new people, I will admit defeat and ask for the name to be repeated. At the point of introduction, all my mental energy is going into the task of smiling and looking agreeable. This, it appears, is such an uphill battle, I'm left with no spare brain capacity. With the result: I can be introduced to people ten or twenty times, over a period of decades, and still not have a clue as to their names.

I will no longer pretend to be an old fan of their work, their company or their product. I acknowledge that it's far more likely that I've become confused, and the thing I've read/seen/heard/bought was done by their arch rival.

I will no longer pretend to have seen the new signs outside David's business. When David tells me he's spent $10 000 re-doing his shop-front, I find myself automatically saying: 'Yes, and doesn't it look great.' I now acknowledge this will inevitably lead David to ask: 'Which bit in particular?'

I will not attempt to wriggle out of David's inquiry by slurring my words and leaving pauses.

- Yes, well I really love the new win ... awn ... doo ...
- Doorway?
- Yes, doorway, especially the way you've surrounded it with ...
- Neons?
- Yes, neons. Exactly. In that wonderful colour. What do you think one would call that colour?
- I think most people would call it 'blue'.

I will no longer offer lengthy and passionate views about the level of violence in the film Gladiator. The point will inevitably be reached where I have to admit I've never seen it.

I will no longer remove my shirt during a social gathering. I now understanding that, while my body may look good in those sunbaking photos, that's because I was (a) horizontal and (b) breathing in. I now accept that (a) vertical and (b) dancing to 'Nutbush City Limits' is another matter entirely.

I will not claim to remember the gender, age and name of everyone's kids. The attempt to ask 'How's the kid(s)?' — with the 's' half-swallowed so they can take their pick about whether they have one kid or ten — is sometimes successful, except when the response is: 'But you know Gary and I are in the IVF program.'

I will not pretend I can hear somebody over the music when I can't. Nor will I take the punt that they are telling me a joke by laughing uproariously the instant I see their mouth stop moving. Especially since it's just as likely they're disclosing details of their fatal disease.

I will no longer pretend to remember the name of Michelle's cousin. Especially as I can't be sure whether it is Judy or Julie. Or maybe June. And there's a very good chance it's Rhonda. I will no longer stage a coughing fit when someone asks to be introduced.

I accept that the length of one's anecdotes should not exceed the amount of time you've known the listener. My hilarious half-hour account of our family boating holiday may be better reserved for old friends.

I will refuse the chicken wings from the proffered tray. Experience teaches there is never anywhere to put the gnawed bone. Except, wrapped in a paper napkin, in one's own pocket. I now accept that this can leave one's dry-cleaner unimpressed.

I will strive to be enigmatic when drunk. No longer will I feel personally responsible to fill every gap in the conversation. Nor will I feel the conversation would go better if someone stood up for the point of view currently being attacked by everyone else in the room. In future: let the next drunk guy do it.

And, finally, but crucially: *I will apologise to everyone.* Just as soon as I can remember their names.

Clash of Wobblies

When deciding to take up any sort of competitive sport, the trick is to find an opponent of similar ability, which is the reason I was patrolling the office, squash racquet in hand, hunting out the sort of emphysemic, pot-bellied lard-legs who'd be my perfect match.

Finally my eyes alighted on this broken-down figure in the corner of the office, the bum amply filling the chair, the belly straining against the elastic expanders in his pants, the hands busy manoeuvring another doughnut towards his mouth. My kind of squash opponent.

To reveal his true name would be too humiliating for the man concerned, so let's just call him 'Tony Squires'.

'Tony Squires' and I met on the court the very next day. And what a sight we made: two overweight men, dressed in very tight shorts, trying to hit the bejesus out of a rubber ball, all the time wondering why our sports gear had shrunk so badly since its last use, sometime in the late 1970s.

Ten minutes into the game, and we'd both turned bright red — the sort of throbbing, alarming red which a paint catalogue might call 'coronary cerise'. Each realised he might die at any minute, but each was spurred on by one bright hope: from the look of things, the other might die first. And then the survivor would win. Sure, the survivor would be crippled for life. Certainly, he'd have the death of a colleague on his conscience. But he'd win. Further proof that within even the most spongy-bottomed male there lingers sufficient aggression to launch World War III.

Consider what happens when a man misses the ball. Does he maturely take note of his error? Does he quietly work on improving his next shot? Not quite. Instead he throws his racquet to the ground and lets loose a scream of bloodcurdling intensity.

Even the most effete man believes his manhood is at stake when he's placed in a competitive situation. That's why we overturn the Squatter board in a blind rage, just because our five-year-old was the first to irrigate his paddocks.

And that's why we lie awake nights, sweating mad over the bastard boss and how we've been passed over for promotion — wondering whether a conviction for first-degree murder might affect our superannuation entitlements.

And so what we lacked in talent, 'Tony Squires' and I were making up for in pure aggression — creating a game which combines the sweet elegance of English squash racquets with the mindless brutality of Rugby League. And, for those of you who play squash, there's nothing quite like the look of wide-eyed surprise on an opponent's face when you first unleash the full power of a head-high tackle.

As 'Tony Squires' may well have asked, save for his momentary lack of consciousness: Why are men so aggressive? Scientists believe it may result from the way the male brain is regularly bathed in a naturally occurring liquid known as 'beer'.

Certainly, men will compete over anything — some even competing with their wives, trying to be the first to finish common household chores, such as orgasm.

What would happen if men could give birth? They'd turn it into a competition: 'You should have seen the bloke in the next labour ward,' they'd say, as they showed their mates their birth video on action replay. 'He was struggling and straining, and out pops this little five-pounder. What a poofter! Mate, mine was a 12-pounder with a 20-hour labour, and we bonded right on touchdown. As for the breast-feeding — it was up with the footy jersey and the little tiger was away.'

As for me, the lungs have recovered, but not the ego. That's what worries me — if 'Tony Squires' can beat me five games to nil, what does it say about the way *I* must look?

8

'So I suppose these don't belong to either of you?' says Jocasta, staring grimly at Batboy and me, as we try to wriggle out of the tightening domestic noose.

'Yeah,' Batboy stammers finally, showing a most regrettable streak of honesty, 'the CD is mine.'

Which leaves Jocasta to focus on me: 'So,' she says with a wave of the size 10½ shoes, 'what about you, Cinderella?'

Clean bowled

'I'm sick of this house, and I'm sick of this idea that if you leave things lying around, *someone* will magically pick them up.' Jocasta is standing in the living room, holding a Smash Mouth CD in one hand and a pair of kicked-off men's shoes, size 10½, in the other.

'So I suppose these don't belong to either of you?' says Jocasta, staring grimly at Batboy and me, as we try to wriggle out of the tightening domestic noose.

'Yeah,' Batboy stammers finally, showing a most regrettable streak of honesty, 'the CD is mine.'

Which leaves Jocasta to focus on me: 'So,' she says with a wave of the shoes, 'what about you, Cinderella?'

'Well,' I say, 'actually I was just about to put them away.'

Jocasta is an attractive woman, but perhaps less so when she is letting loose a snort of derision at one's expense. It's time to go into major damage control, and I quickly suggest we all hop in.

'It'll be fine,' I say soothingly, speaking as one would to a madman wired with explosive. 'I'll take all the stuff out of all the kitchen cupboards and scrub them down, and then I'll restack and refold everything in the linen cupboard.'

Pretty helpful offer, I think you'll agree. And yet what do I get? Another snort.

'That's typical,' says Jocasta. 'You always want to do these major jobs, these show-offy, once-a-year sort of jobs, and you never want to do the ordinary, boring, once-a-week jobs, like cleaning the bathroom.'

My mind grinds and clunks as I wonder exactly *why* I don't like doing the ordinary, boring, grungy jobs and suddenly, despite myself, the truth comes tumbling out: 'Well, I guess nobody does.'

It's an admission which leaves me, about three minutes later, being loaded-up with cleaning products and a strict instruction to have the entire bathroom spotless by noon.

This poses a problem for the supposedly aware man — how to successfully complete the allotted task without confessing that, in all your forty years, you've never actually cleaned a whole bathroom. Certainly, it seems a mistake to ask how it's done, so I just head in there with anything I can find labelled 'cleaning product'. If Jif doesn't do the job, I'll give it a blast with oven-cleaner.

As it happens, after a while I actually start becoming involved in the job. There are some grey bits in the grouting which I get off with a scratchy pad, and some mess around the water spout which I manage to get off by unscrewing the tap. Then there's the toilet, which to be cleaned properly needs the whole seat assembly unscrewed and removed, which I find pretty easy, especially using my battery drill, fitted with its screwdriver attachment, and with a little squirt of WD40 on the bolt heads and some bricklayer's acid on the cement joints.

It is then Jocasta comes in to find me hunched over my tool box — the bathroom a disaster, the taps on the floor, the toilet disassembled — wearing my tool belt and, in order to use the acid, my full-face safety breathing apparatus.

'I can't believe,' said Jocasta, aghast, 'the way you've managed to turn the ultimate ordinary job into a show-off bloke's job. I suppose you were worried your male appendage would drop off if you actually did it properly?' (Only she didn't say 'male appendage'.)

I could see her argument, but in such circumstances the old marital advice holds true: the best form of defence is attack.

'Well, I don't know who's been *trying* to clean this bathroom for the past ten years,' I say, rather gamely, 'but they haven't been doing a very thorough job.'

A week later, with the benefit of considerable time on my own for contemplation, I now see this comment was a mistake. A mistake which led directly to Jocasta's latest idea: the Household Tasks Roster, stuck up there on the fridge door. Revenge, I discover, belongs to she who allocates the jobs.

The new roster, posted yesterday, distributes jobs for the next eight weeks. Eight weeks in which I will be able, in Jocasta's words, 'to clean the bathroom to your own high standards — something that should give you enormous personal satisfaction.'

For Batboy and The Space Cadet, the roster affords different opportunities. Opportunities — again in Jocasta's words — for them to 'perhaps learn the skills that may make you the world's first two reasonable men and thus improve the life of some other poor benighted woman.'

And for herself? Jocasta's new roster counsels eight weeks of 'quiet hand-watering of the garden', sufficient time, she says, for her to get over the image of her husband, the tool box, and the bathroom.

Pies de Resistance

The annual *Good Food Guide* is always full of top-shelf nosheries which attract a very sophisticated and cosmopolitan set. But whatever happened to the establishments attended by the rest of us?

Susan's Sandwich Bar

This popular city haunt has now reopened after last year's embarrassing health scare, and manageress–owner Susan declares the whole place is now 'absolutely' rodent-free. Customers can enjoy the delicate ambience created by the fusion of city bus fumes and decades of hot-oil frying, all combined with Susan's own unmistakable personal *parfum* — 'a really quite staggering mix', in the words of one regular.

A display of produce, plucked fresh each morning from Susan's very own freezer, is presented in a glass-topped counter — much of it completely free of botulism. Customers can choose from an array of traditional sandwich fillings, safe in the knowledge that exotic hints of sardine and salami will be added via Susan's tongs. Which is not to underrate the more subtle contributions of her chief assistant, Terry, and his garlic breath — giving that unmistakable *je ne sais quoi* to everything he serves.

Susan's personal recommendation is her bestselling meat pie — so structurally unsound that it always ends up all over the diner's shirt. Chuckles Terry with a mischievous grin: 'Our pies are like Armani suits — all the best people end up wearing them.'

Susan's is open from 7.30 a.m. until Terry's feet start hurting, normally about 5.45 p.m.

Barry Chow's All-You-Can-Eat Chinese Restaurant

The Good Food Guide restaurants may be terrific on quality, but Barry Chow's the man for pure quantity. It's the first choice for all those of us who judge a meal principally on its weight.

But Barry also knows the All-You-Can-Eat Restaurant walks a narrow line. If the neon signs outside suggest endless helpings, then it's up to the food itself to encourage some sort of moderation. And indeed it does — a first serving of Barry's Mongolian lamb usually being enough to sober up the most enthusiastic of diners. 'I couldn't eat another thing,' say the testimonials plastered on Barry's window — quotes often recorded as customers ran screaming for the door.

'There's nothing like my spring rolls,' says Barry, as he turns up the blinding fluorescent lighting and the 2KY radio call, 'for ensuring a good flow-through of customers.'

The Factory Canteen

A place so popular that the same customers come day after day, largely because no other food is available within 10 kilometres.

Says head chef, Mike: 'It's a lie that all our chefs learned their cooking skills in "the Big House". At least *one* could cook before his prison sentence. Besides,' he adds with a wink, 'at least they're used to cooking for a captive market.'

Betty's Family Restaurant and Steak Bar

Here the word 'family' is used in its traditional Australian sense, as in 'family room', 'family holiday' and 'family film'. In other words, 'bloody awful'.

In terms of decor, Betty's guiding word has been 'unbreakable', while in terms of cuisine she says her main influences can be summed up in the words 'portion control'.

Better still, everything is microwaved. 'How else could you serve food that's boiling hot on the outside and ice-cold on the inside?' asks Betty, as she pours in another bucket of meat-extender. 'I like to think it lends every dish the glamour and adventure of a bombe Alaska.'

Mum and Dad's

This establishment remains so popular that many Sydneysiders choose it for their meal every night of the week. On my most recent visit, which was last night, I again chose the lamb chops with mash and Brussels sprouts, while my companion opted for the lamb chops with mash and Brussels sprouts.

Meanwhile, our two younger companions toyed with the lamb chops, tried to hide the sprouts under the bones, and cried when they weren't allowed to watch *South Park*. Service is unfussy, with a hint of the colourful Latin should patrons decline to take their chairs with speed. The ambience is informal, with patrons encouraged to fetch their own drinks during the course of the meal and, indeed, to wash up afterwards.

Some young diners have complained of the chef's violent temper, often occasioned by a refusal to consume the Brussels sprouts. Most, however, agree that this is more than made up for by the price.

Mum and Dad's is free (although, some patrons warn, you'll be paying for the rest of your life).

The Politically Correct Jokebook

Some people claim that the only funny joke is a politically incorrect one — one that's racist, or sexist or just plain mean.

Maybe the plain mean part is correct. As to the rest, you've just got to pick deserving targets. Welcome to the Politically Correct Jokebook.

Part 1: Bankers

Why do Australian bankers describe themselves as 'terrific housekeepers'?
– Because if things become messy, they get to keep the house.

Why did the bank customer cross the road?
– To try and find the end of the queue.

Why is a bank customer like a seagull?
– Because you can make 500 deposits on a car, and still not be the one who owns it.

Why is a bank customer like a bank robber?
– Because, if she ever demands money at the counter, she'll be subject to serious charges.

Why are the Australian banks like the members of an infantry battalion?
– Because, on a secret signal, they all start charging at the same time.

Why are the four major banks like a symphony orchestra?
– Because they are so used to acting in concert.

Why are Australian banks like Cold War spies?
– Because, even under torture, they'll give nothing away.

Why did the shark off Bondi circle the banker but never attack?
– Professional respect.

Why are Australian banks like the Israeli army?
– Because they both employ counter-terrorists.

What's the difference between any Australian banker and your teenage son?
– None. Neither has paid you any interest for years.

Why is an Australian banker like a pelican?
– Because the first thing you notice is the enormous size of the bill.

What do call a banker when he's selling you a new loan?
– Con.

What do you call a bank customer whose got nothing on her bank statement except charges?
– Fiona.

What do you call a banker at a farm repossession?
– Rich.

What do you call a bank customer whose just had his vehicle repossessed?
– Carlos.

Why are bankers like bushrangers?
– Because they've holed up in small towns, taken everyone's money, and then shot through in a hurry.

Banker, banker! Everyone in this bank keeps ignoring me!
– Next please.

Banker, banker! I've only got 59 seconds to pay in this cheque, or you get to repossess my farm.
– Hold on a minute, please.

Knock Knock,
Who's there?
A teller.
A teller who?
Ateller the Hun.

Why are bank-loan officers like grave diggers?
– Because they dig the hole for you, then help you in.

Part 2: Race-card politicians

There's a point where the politics are so pathetic, and the national shame so great, there's only one sensible response: create some schoolyard jokes. Thus part two of our Politically Correct Jokebook.

What do you call the Australian Prime Minister when he's visiting an Aboriginal neighbourhood?
– Lost.

What do you call the Australian Prime Minister when he's visiting the United Nations?
– The defendant.

Why is the Australian Prime Minister like a drug runner?
– Because he's afraid to be judged by international customs.

How many Darwin magistrates does it take to change a light bulb?
– They don't bother. They've got no power anyway.

Why is a racist like a drunk?
– Because everything he says ends in a slur.

Why are Australian politicians like Old Sydney Town?
– Both offer a variety of 18th-century views.

What's the difference between a black child stealing a truck, and a truck arriving to steal a black child?
– Only one's a crime: the one in which the black child knows where he's going.

Why is the Northern Territory Chief Minister like an Australian bank?
– Because the rest of the country constantly gives him money, but he never pays any interest.

Why didn't the racist cross the road?
– Because he didn't want to see the other side.

Why did the Government gag parliamentary debate on the Northern Territory?
– Because only people in jail should finish their sentences.

Why did the Liberal cross the floor of Parliament?
– Because 98 per cent of her party were giving the rest a bad name.

Why was the Government happy to intervene over Northern Territory's euthanasia laws, but not over the Territory's mandatory sentencing laws?
– Because it only wants to encourage suicide among young people.

Why is a bigot like the announcer at Rosehill Racecourse?
– Because they both start shouting the instant they see a new race.

Have you heard about the politician who discovered a new tax that is actually popular?
– It's attacks on black Australians.

What's the difference between stealing a black child and stealing a packet of biscuits.
– None. Whichever gets stolen, the black child does the time.

Why does St Vincent's heart-transplant team only use the hearts of Cabinet ministers?
– They prefer ones that have never been used.

Why did the black child steal correcting fluid.
– Because he saw it was called White Out.

How many Prime Ministers does it take to change a light bulb?
– None. That light bulb worked fine in 1956, so why change it now.

Inviting Trouble

I'm standing at the frypan, pushing around some slabs of steak, while I consider precisely how to put the question. Finally I sing-song it over my shoulder: 'The office party is on in a couple of weeks; do you think you'll want to come along?'

I am trying to sound upbeat, positive, like a man who can think of nothing better than to take his partner to his office party. But deep in the back of my head, I can hear a treacherous little voice mumbling: 'Hope she says no.'

Now this is interesting, because it raises a question: why would a happily-partnered person, especially one armed with The Belly, want to attend his office party without his partner?

And the answer — and I am shocked when I tease it forth from the swamp that is my subconscious — can only be one thing. Women.

Somewhere my brain is harbouring some sort of pathetic fantasy whereby I trundle into the office Christmas party, wearing the fresh polyester shirt, the dab of Blue Stratos behind the ears, and various women will attempt to get into my pants. Which will be pretty amazing, since it's pretty damn tight in here already.

But men like to maintain hope. However middle-aged, however ungainly in appearance, however happily married, however guilty we know we'd feel ... we always want to think it's at least possible. In theory.

What do we think is actually going to happen? By what bizarre miracle do we think women, who as a group have not shown us a second glance for a decade, are suddenly going to overcome their aversion?

The answer — and I think I speak for all men here — is nuclear war. We know that one night — maybe in a year, maybe in fifty — the announcement will be made that the world is about to be destroyed in a nuclear hellfire, and this, we fondly imagine, may cause women everywhere to reach hurriedly for whatever man happens to be handy. And when it happens we want to be the one sitting next to Monica from dispatch.

Which brings the festive season problem: how to stop your partner coming to your office Christmas party (and sitting herself between you and Monica) without actually saying she can't come. Hence our dinner-time discussion:

Me: 'So do you want to come to the party?'

Jocasta: 'Oh, I don't care. If you want me to, I will.'

Me: 'Well, I'd love you to; it would be great, although — from your point of view — I guess it will be full of all those, you know, office types.'

Jocasta: 'You're trying to talk me out of going, aren't you?'

Me (sweating): 'No, honest, no.'

Jocasta (striding towards me, with scissors): 'You want to go on your own, eh, Don Juan? Just so you can get

226

your mitts on some poor deluded woman. Well, I think it's pathetic.'

This conversation represents your basic worst-case scenario, whereby your partner instantly cancels all engagements in order to attend your office party and, if possible, also invites her mother.

The problem is that your spouse never believes the truth, which is: all you want to do is flirt. All married people, both men and women, are like this: we want to walk into a party, go up to other married people of the opposite sex, and attempt to create some sexual electricity. Just to see if it can still be done. It's like turning on an old valve radio. It's not that you want to listen to the programs; you just want to check if it still goes.

And so you have these weird, breathy discussions with complete strangers:

Man: 'Yes, well, we tried the Laminex top and found it quite hard-wearing, especially in heavy wear areas.'

Woman: 'Yes, we used to have Laminex, but then Patrick and I changed over to the Corian benchtops. Which are great.'

And all through this, you'll be sort of leaning towards each other slightly, both of you sucking in your tummies and going all moony in the eyes.

Naturally nothing is going to happen. You are two middle-aged parents, with mortgages and families. Finding a spare five minutes to pay the gas bill is a minor miracle, never mind taking off a whole morning for a torrid affair.

And so, after about thirty minutes, you'll both wander off, a strange tingle in your head, thrilling to your shock discovery: 'I AM STILL ATTRACTIVE TO THE OPPOSITE SEX! (Even if only when the OPPOSITE SEX is very DRUNK because it's CHRISTMAS).'

But still Jocasta remains suspicious. And now, of course, she wants to come to my party. Especially, she says, as her work party will be really dull, full of 'office types'.

She's suggested I shouldn't even bother going to her bash. Apparently, I'd only be bored. It's wonderful, isn't it, how she always puts my welfare first?

Griswold's Christmas

Frank, over the road, has installed some Christmas lights, strung across the front of his house. They twinkle merrily. On Saturday I visit Target, to check out the prices. Outdoor Christmas lights cost $65, and I make the purchase.

When I get home, Jocasta is not happy. She says $65 is a lot of money, plus there's all the electricity. She mentions the *National Lampoon* film in which Chevy Chase played Clark Griswold — a daggy American whose dedication to Christmas illuminations results in the conflagration of his own home. She also states that decorating the outside of a suburban house with lights is a bit 'goofy'. (And this from a woman who last month purchased an item of garden statuary.)

I'm used to this sort of abuse. With quiet dignity, I turn on my heels and proceed outside to string my lights. I don't want to go on about it, but I did a pretty amazing job — creating several Christmas-tree shapes across the front of our house before the line of lights ran out.

Jocasta didn't get to see the effect straight away. We drove off before it was dark, heading for Carols by Candlelight two suburbs away. These ones are down on the bay, and the carols aren't the only attraction. The houses fronting the park have been done up with lights and decorations. And all the way there, Jocasta is calling me Clark Griswold. 'You'll be able to pick up a few tips for next year, Clark. That's if our house isn't a smouldering ruin by the time we get home.'

It's a real scene down at the park. There's a couple of hundred people singing carols, and as dusk falls, all the household lights come on. They've been at this for decades, and fierce competition has sprung up. Everyone is going for a different look, and Jocasta pokes me in the ribs with each new concept: a model Santa climbing onto a roof, a line of cut-out elves, even a householder who has dressed in a Santa suit to add a live element to his display. 'Now, there's an idea for you, Clark,' she says, giving me a squeeze. 'Perfect body for it.'

The next house along has gone for the religious look — beautiful glass models of Joseph and Mary, lit from within. Next up, there's Vegas — a house throbbing with lights. 'Compared to that, Clark, your effort is a bit like Reno — fewer lights, and a bit further west.'

She's trying to be ironic and detached, but I know my Jocasta. Ever so slowly, she's becoming taken with the idea. 'So, tell me again,' she says, finally, 'how much is each extra set of lights?'

We come around the corner, and a particularly big crowd is in front of one house. There's much excited talking and pointing. It's hard to imagine what the householder has done to create such interest. Already we've seen every imaginable permutation: toy trains with elves aboard, electric angels singing hymns, cut-out reindeer teams spread over two front yards.

We peek through the crowd, and then we understand. It's a manger scene, constructed in the front garden. There's a patch of 'snow' — white polystyrene cubes covering the ground — and a thatched roof to indicate the manger. A three-year-old girl sits cross-legged in a beautiful white dress, her hair specially curled and coiffured. She is spotlit. Next to her, on the ground: a crib. In the crib — and I swear I'm not making this up — A REAL BABY.

The baby is tiny enough that it is still sucking on the back of its hand. It's probably about nine weeks old. It's pretty much the most bizarre thing I've ever seen.

Back on the street corner, two Mr Whippy vans have pulled up, and are doing a roaring trade. They know a real attraction when they see it. The blokes down the road might be burning three hundred bucks worth of power each night, but without a real baby ...

The mother is on the porch, checking on the children, but she keeps clear of the limelight. It's just the main players. The sister. The baby. The white polystyrene snow. I must say they look quite happy. That little Lord Jesus, no crying he makes.

Suddenly, I realise the sort of competition I've got myself into. It may start with $65 at Target, but victory takes so much more.

We get home, our new lights twinkling, and Jocasta lets out a little sigh of pleasure. She's even stopped calling me Clark. It seems Jocasta is converted, but I'm left wandering just how serious she is about us having something *special* for next year. I consult my calender and calculator, then throw a casual arm around her: 'How about a weekend away, just the two of us, about March 25?'

The Christmas Cheer

Here's what should happen on Christmas Day:

9.15 a.m. Awake to share perfect presents with perfect family.

12 noon Sit down to light but varied meal. Discuss world affairs. Enjoy single glass of semillon.

3.20 p.m. Retire with selection of Penguin Classics given by thoughtful relatives. The Balzac, you discover, is particularly good.

I don't know about your place, but here is what is more likely to occur at ours:

5.17 a.m. The Space Cadet runs into bedroom. Debate ensues over precise meaning of the word 'morning'. Allow him to look in Santa stocking. Discover stocking contains half the sugar production of Queensland in easily digestible form.

5.25 a.m. Marvel at the effect of sugar on the young human. Suggest he plays 'somewhere else'.

5.34 a.m. Attempt to re-erect Christmas tree, clearing away all breakages.

6.15 a.m. Help Space Cadet unwrap presents. Explain Santa forgot batteries for the Action Explorer Belt Kit.

6.30 a.m. Suggest Space Cadet jumps into your bed and goes back to sleep.

6.31 a.m. Realise this would have been less painful if he'd first removed the Action Explorer Belt Kit.

6.32 a.m. Remove embedded pieces of Action Explorer Belt Kit from own body. Apply Band-Aids.

6.45 a.m. Fall asleep.

6.46 a.m. Awakened by Batboy. Suggest he might open Santa stocking. Marvel at the effect of sugar on the pre-teen body. Suggest he quietly opens his presents, and allows you to sleep.

6.50 a.m. Awake to sound of the Regurgitator CD being played very loud. Curse Santa for his musical taste.

6.57 a.m. Disassemble both CD player and son. Return to bed and sleep.

7.00 a.m. Awakened by Jocasta, who says she 'slept like a log' but is now ready for her cup of tea. Stomp down hall and prepare tea, impaling self on several pieces of the Action Explorer Belt Set.

7.05 a.m. Take Jocasta tea and breakfast on tray, walking in with tray held high, displaying the skills learnt when working as a waiter at the Hilton. Smile indulgently as Jocasta says: 'Stop showing off or it will end up all over me.'

7.06 a.m. Help Jocasta out of bed and bathe injured and burnt areas. Change sheets. Suggest you both might as well open presents now.

7.15 a.m. Open presents and immediately use/wear/eat anything that is opened.

7.25 a.m. Sit in new tropical shirt, matched by fresh Ugh boots, listening to Batboy's Regurgitator album, while eating panforte and watching new Elvis video. Does pleasure get any more intense than this?

9.00 a.m. Realise Ughies are becoming a trifle warm, Elvis movie is over, and that your early consumption of panforte is creating waves of nausea.

9.05 a.m. Prepare sit-down dinner for 15 relatives, discussing how to avoid usual tensions between Grandfather Ryan and Uncle Steve. Decide lots of alcohol will 'probably help them relax'.

9.30 a.m. Begin preparation of own fancy-pants show-off dish, congratulating self for being so well prepared.

9.55 a.m. Turn page in cookbook and see 'Step 7: soak beans for 7 hours, then refrigerate overnight.' Throw book on floor and weep.

10.00 a.m. Decide to pour brandy onto pudding. Decide to test brandy 'just to make sure it's not gone off'.

10.05 a.m. Remain unsure about quality of brandy. Test again.

10.15 a.m. One can't take too many precautions before one serves to guests . . .

12.15 p.m. Welcome relatives, staggering slightly. Open oven and realise turkey is in traditional shape: stuffed.

12.30 p.m. Share presents with relatives. Tell sister: 'I wanted this book from the moment it came out.' Fail to disclose: 'That's why I bought it three months ago.'

12.45 p.m. Help Space Cadet assemble kid's tent he's been given by grandparents.

12.50 p.m. Realise why shops are closed on Christmas Day. Not for religious reasons, but so you can't complain they forgot to pack the tent pegs.

1.05 p.m. Serve four-course meal in 35-degree heat, with wide range of traditional thirst quenchers such as red wine and whiskey.

1.30 p.m. During pudding, casually introduce topic of funny old family rift — the one that everyone used to be so 'thingy' about, but now can all have a good laugh over.

1.40 p.m. Discover family not at the 'good laugh' stage quite yet.

1.45 p.m. Use broken piece of Action Explorer Belt to separate Uncle Mark from Pa. Use fire extinguisher on tree. And turkey.

2.00 p.m. Stagger towards room with copy of new Bryce Courtenay novel. Discover it's beyond you.

5.00 p.m. Wake up. Apologise. Share out left-overs.

5.10 p.m. Watch amazed as Uncle Mark complains that pubs are forced to close on Christmas Day. 'I mean they let the *churches* open — so it's just another damn double standard.'

7.00 p.m. Farewell guests, and discover the meaning of 'Christmas cheer'. It's the yell that goes up when it's all over.

In Bed with Jocasta

The Space Cadet is in the back seat, crying — not the bunged-on hysteria he sometimes employs to get his own way, but the painful, broken sobbing of a boy who has come to a sudden and shattering realisation: that his father is a total joke. Jocasta is in the passenger seat, staring stonily ahead, no doubt wondering how she, a woman who once had some choices in life, has ended up here — in this car, with this man, in this town.

The town is Geurie, a dusty one-pubber just east of Dubbo, in western New South Wales — and we're parked in the long grass out the back of the pub, nestled in beside the stack of smashed empties. It is dusk, and I've just explained my big plan for the night: that we sleep the night right here, all four of us, under a borrowed blanket in the back of the family station-wagon, using our T-shirts as pillows.

Somehow they are not impressed. I don't know why. I've already seen the publican and borrowed the blanket. It's a sort of a prickly ex-army thing, but it's better than nothing. And nothing is what's been on offer at the twenty-three pubs we've already tried — all of them refusing us a bed as they tried to cope with an unlikely influx of vacationers, railway workers and reps.

My problem is that Jocasta, sitting grimly silent, is equipped with an unbeatable 'I told you so', a gold-plated, Exocet missile of an 'I told you so'. Before we left, she'd rung every pub and motel on the road to Dubbo. She'd thoroughly established the lack of vacancies, and said we should postpone our trip.

That's when I made what, in retrospect, was my unwise rejoinder. 'Don't be stupid — who'd go to Dubbo? We're sure to get a bed.'

Back behind the pub, I unpack the car in the gathering dusk, trying to imagine how we'll all fit — two adults, Batboy and the always wriggly Space Cadet. 'It'll be an adventure,' I say with a hollow brightness.

I watch Jocasta's face, and for a moment it looks as though she's going to say it — that 'I told you so'. But she holds her fire. And, as every spouse knows, nothing's so terrifying as an 'I told you so' held in abeyance — lying there between you, softly ticking.

The Space Cadet is still weeping. Between sobs, he explains how we will almost certainly get killed by robbers, who will come up while we are asleep and stare at us through the windows, their evil noses pressed to the glass.

Jocasta agrees that my plan may result in murder. Considering the level of provocation, she'd probably only have to serve a year of the sentence. Finally she speaks, and it's something even tougher than the 'I told you so'. What she says is: 'It's like your whole petrol-tank thing.'

That's how unreasonable Jocasta can be. Just because we happen to be sitting in a motionless car in the gathering dusk, she has to mention every other time we've sat in a motionless car in the gathering dusk — even though they're unrelated. (This time: because I thought we'd find a hotel. The last time: because I thought we'd find a petrol station.)

I tell The Space Cadet I'll hang our towels over all the windows so the robbers can't see us. He says: 'I knew there were robbers here — and you said there weren't.' The sobs come harder.

Jocasta adopts that far-away philosophical look, and I know she's going to call me by a really dirty name. Yep — here it comes — I'm 'a man'.

'It's something about men, isn't it?' she says, finally. 'You're just totally convinced the world's been built for your personal convenience. And that's why you drive around with the needle on empty. You're certain there'll be a petrol station just when you run out. Or that somehow you'll get a bed.'

No way was I going to let her get away with that. It wasn't as if I wasn't prepared for every contingency. I'd even packed two bottles of Hunter shiraz — long favoured as an aid to sleeping in the back of a station-wagon. But it's those acts of thoughtfulness that never get a mention.

'Actually, I think it's good,' says Jocasta. 'Sleeping here might finally teach you a lesson: that things don't always turn out right.'

The night darkens with a big-sky sunset glowing red on the horizon — everything quiet save for the boy's rhythmic sobbing. Then I spot him — the publican walking briskly towards the car. It's all I need. He probably wants his blanket back.

He addresses Jocasta: 'Ah, I just can't let you all sleep out here — it would be terrible with two young ones.' His eighteen-year-old son can sleep on a spare bed in his sister's room. We can have the boy's bedroom.

Somehow, miraculously, things have turned out for the best. We wander inside, and all leap into the son's huge water bed, laughing and giggling.

I know I'll rot in hell, but I can't resist it as I lean close, and whisper the sweet words. 'Jocasta ... I told you so.'

I am in bed with Jocasta, and things couldn't be better.